BIBLIOGRAPHICAL BULLETIN

TABLE OF CONTENTS

1. EDITORIAL INTRODUCTION

The intended aim of *Afroasiatic Linguistics* is not only to serve as an outlet for linguistic articles dealing with topics within the domain of the Afroasiatic languages, but also to reflect recent developments in the field in general. Therefore, we consider it essential to publish reviews of books and articles that have appeared elsewhere. As far as books are concerned, we are extending our invitation to Publishers to put *AAL* on their list of reviewing journals. Here I would like to express my gratitude to Mouton Publishers, and to Mr. Paul M. Waszink of Mouton in particular, for their cooperation and immediate response to our request for review copies of their publications. In addition to the ones appearing in the present fascicle, some more of Mouton's monographs will be reviewed in the near future.

Since our chief purpose is to provide a channel for discussion of ongoing research in the field, whatever the format or size of the publications, the Bibliographical Bulletin will include reviews or notices of articles as well as of books. It often happens that specialists of a field read articles on topics close to their hearts and may have some objections or additions that, by themselves, would not justify the writing of a full-length article. In

such cases, short notices of reviews summing up the content of the articles reviewed and
further voicing the reviewers' own ideas about the same subject would be most welcomed by the
Editors of this journal. The reviews of articles in this issue were all solicited — only in
order to set a precedent. It is hoped that in the future scholars will volunteer such notes
or reviews after having read articles which are of special interest to them. We encourage
discussions and debates on these pages.

Naturally, reviewers carry the responsibility for the opinions expressed by them. Replies,
rejoinders are invited.

R. H.

*2. COMPARATIVE STUDIES

2.1   **(Survey Article)**
Le chamito-sémitique et les langues africaines (En marge de l'étude de J. Tubiana)
By Karel Petráček (Prague)

2.1.1. LE CHAMITO-SÉMITIQUE ET LES AUTRES LANGUES DANS LE MONDE

Pendant l'histoire riche des études chamito-sémitiques on a essayé plusieurs fois d'étudier
les relations de ces langues comme une unité, ou partiellement avec les langues différentes,
parlées en Europe, en Asie, en OCÉANIE, en POLYNÉSIE (MacDonald 1889,1894,1896,1899,1901,1907,
voir la critique négative par M.Cohen,1947,27;Schröder,1929;Gelb,*AJSL* 47,140-1;O'Grady 1971,
780 parle de plusieurs travaux) et en AMÉRIQUE[1] [Leedsberg,1903; Harris,1944 montre bien le
danger de comparaison des traits typologiques entre le sémitique et la langue des Yocuts]
Notons encore l'idée bien curieuse de mettre les langues chamito-sémitiques (sémitiques) en
comparaison avec le CHINOIS (Honorat,1933,rejeté par Guidi, *RSO* 15,107). En Europe (ou en
Eurasie) c'étaient le plus souvent LES LANGUES ANCIENNES DE LA GRANDE BRETAGNE (Pokorny,1951,
Wagner,1959,Rössler-Wagner,1960,Isserlin,1970,Adams,1970), LES LANGUES CAUCASIENNES (Trombetti,
1902-3,Marr,1908,van Ginneken,1938,1939a,1939b; la bibliographie chez Polák,1950;v.aussie Gar-
bini,1972,120), LES LANGUES DRAVIDIENNES dans le subcontinent indien (Kluge,1947,Homburger,
1949b,1954,1960-3 etc.,Lahovary,1963), LE BASQUE (Gabelentz,1893,Mukarovsky,1964,1966a,1966b,
1966-7,1969a,1969b,1972) et surtout LES LANGUES INDO-EUROPÉNNES directement (Delitzsch,1873,
Moeller,1909,1911,1920,Pedersen,1927,Meriggi,1927,Schott,1936 etc., plus récemment voir
Heilmann,1949,Brunner,1969,Fraenkel,1970,Schenkel,1971; les opinions des sémitisants M.Cohen,
1933-1955,185,Gelb,1969,XII,Moscati et al.,1964,17,17,W.von Soden,1973,16;Voegelin 1964,281 en
termes de la linguistique des "phyla"; Vycichl,1974 dans une perspective typologique), puis
dans le cadre de la théorie NOSTRATIQUE ANCIENNE (Cuny,1924,1935-8,1930,1943,1946) et NOUVELLE
(Dolgopolskij,1964,1968,1971,Illič-Svityč,1971a,1971b,1964,1967,v.aussi Skalička,1974). Les
protagonistes de la théorie d'une MONOGENÈSE DE TOUTES LES LANGUES DANS LE MONDE (Trombetti,
1905,1923; la théorie japhétique et stadiale de Marr,1933,1933-4,la doctrine nouvelle de
Měščaninov,1936,1940,1950 - pour les deux v.Zvegincev,1960,228-9) ont émis plusieurs hypothèses où le chamito-sémitique étoit représenté.

Une autre théorie de la monogenèse est fondée sur la GLOTTOCHRONOLOGIE de M.Swadesh. Ce qui
nous intéresse de ses douze groupes conçus comme des familles apparentées génétiquement
(Landar,1966,162), ce sont seulement ceux qui sont les plus proches du chamito-sémitique
(afroasiatique) en Afrique et en Eurasie: les groupes 6.12.,les autres (1.-4.) étant répartis
en Océanie et en Amérique. Il est utile de les présenter sous la forme du graphe (1960 - cité ici;
1964,1971). Les relations chronologiques (en minimum de siècles) sont indiquées dans le tableau
(seulement pour les langues 8.-12.). Pour le GRAPHE et le TABLEAU voir à la fin de notre
exposé.

La glottochronologie n'est pas sans doute sans problèmes. Mais les procédés lexico-statistiques ont été introduits dans une large mesure même dans la subclassification des langues chamito-sémitiques où les données tirées des autres langues ne manquaient pas, mais sans interprétation génétique (Murtonen,1969,1974,Bender,1971,1973,1974; sur la bibliographie v.Fronzaroli,1973). L'évaluation chronologique est mise en question même dans le domaine chamito-sémitique (Bender, 1972).

L'application de la thèse de la monogenèse dans les termes de Swadesh (et Sapir) se trouve chez Voegelin(1964). Son importance consiste dans le fait qu'elle rend possible de voir les relations graduelles entre les langues.

Comme on peut observer, les travaux rapprochant les langues chamito-sémitiques des autres langues (familles de langues) dans le monde en dehors du continent africain et l'Asie de l'Ouest, ont été dirigés avant Swadesh non seulement vers l'Asie, mais aussi vers les autres continents (l'Océanie, l'Amérique et la zone du basque). On voulait alors comparer les langues chamito-sémitiques avec les langues de tous les continents du monde. En somme, ces théories sont en accord avec les tâches des "monogénétistes" (Trombetti,Swadesh); mais les méthodes sont naturellement différentes.

Pour le moment, nous n'avons pas besoin de critiquer ces théories et, notre terrain étant plus restreint, nous nous bornons seulement à ce résumé bibliographique. On peut dire qu'il est possible dans ce moment de supposer avec une probabilité plus ou moins évident les relations du chamito-sémitique surtout avec les langues dans les continents les plus proches, en Afrique, en Asie de l'Ouest et peut-être aussi en Eurasie (indo-européennes etc.). Il s'agit donc des recherches AFROEURASIATIQUES ayant leur précurseur dans la théorie nostratique.

2.1.2.   LE CHAMITO-SÉMITIQUE ET LES LANGUES AFRICAINES

Le terrain le plus sûr pour la comparaison des langues chamito-sémitiques paraît être dans la proximité géographique, c'est-dire en Afrique. On a élaboré ici plusieurs hypothèses sur les grands problèmes de la classification des langues africaines qui touchent aussi le chamito-sémitique(p.ex. le problème du nilo-hamitique (chari-nile) paranilotique,le problème "tchado-hamitique", le problème nilo-saharien etc.).

2.1.2.1.   L'étude de J.Tubiana

Sous le titre "Le chamito-sémitique et les langues africaines" notre confrère J.Tubiana a publié (1974) une étude qui attire de nouveau l'intérêt des linguistes sur les rapports du chamito-sémitique avec les langues en Afrique, qui sont loin d'être éclaircis. "L'exploration ne devrait pas se limiter au 'tchadohamitique', mais inclure des langues géographiquement plus proches du domaine chamito-sémitique africain, telles les langues du groupe dit 'Saharien central' (...) qui avec le kanuri, nous rapprochent géographiquement du Lac Tchad. Il ne faudrait pas non plus négliger le maba et les langues voisines de celui-ci."

J.Tubiana appuie cette opinion sur ses analyses partielles du plan phonologique où il traite certains problèmes: ḍ cacuminal (occlusive apico-palatale,91), ton distinctif (94), l'étude comparée du lexique visant la constance des correspondances phonologiques (97).

Les matériaux sont tirés le plus souvent du sémitique éthiopien, du sémitique en général, du couchitique et tchadique, puis des langues du Sahara central (têda,daza,kanuri,des dialectes bēRi bideyat et zagha-wa) et de la langue des anciens sultans du Wadday maba.

Les autres problèmes discutés dans l'étude touchent la méthodologie du comparativisme chamito-sémitique et la phonologie chamito-sémitique (les "emphatiques," les labiovelaires,ḍ cacuminal et sa recherche en sémitique,le ton distinctif).

Donc, il ne s'agit pas d'une étude monographique du problème indiqué dans le titre, mais plutôt d'une invitation ou encouragement pour ceux qui s'intéressent aux études historiques et comparées hors du domaine traditionnel du chamito-sémitique. Cet appel doit être suivi, sa force est garantie par les vastes connaissances de J.Tubiana dans plusieurs langues et familles de langues en Afrique, comme le couchitique, l'éthiopien, les langues du Sahara central (zaghawa) où il a fait (avec M.-J.Tubiana et d'autres) les enquêtes dans le cadre d'une mission importante (v.Dossiers;Tubiana,1954,1958-9,1959,1960,1962,1963,1968-9,1970,1974; Tubiana M.-J.et J.,1961,1968).

2.1.2.2. Le diapason des rapprochements

Pour compléter le tableau des relations étudiées entre les langues chamito-sémitiques et les autres langues en Afrique, nous pouvons ajouter ses autres extensions: les rapports supposés avec les langues BANTOUES (Drexel,1934 et les travaux de Meinhof;seulement pour le couchitique Whiteley,1960, Ehret,1974, Dolgopolskij,1973,27; discussion chez Zaborski,1975), avec le PEUL (Meinhof,1910,1911,1922a,1922b,1930), LE MÉROÏTIQUE (la bibliographie et discussion chez Palmer,1970, Greenberg,1971, Vycichl,1973), le BARYA Bender,1968), les langues NILO-HAMITIQUES[2] [Hohenberger,1955, 1956, 1958a, 1958b, voir de W.Leslau, 1961, de Greenberg,1957; sur le problème du groupe nilo-hamitique voir Greenberg,1966,85 ss.,43 ss.,1971,241 ss., Tucker-Bryan,1956,1966, Bryan-Tucker,1948, Ehret,1971, Meeussen,1957, discussion chez Zaborski,1975, Voegelin,1964, Huntingford,1956]. Notons la tâche de Castellino (1962) de rapprocher les systèmes verbaux en chamito-sémitique et les autres langues "négro-africaines" (peul,tchadique, teso,bantu), ainsi que de comparaisons étendues de Mlle Homburger (1928,1939,1949a,1949b,1954, 1955,1957,1960-3), les thèses anciennes de Reinisch (1873) et nouvelles de R.Stopa (1969,1972) sur les rapports supposés de certaines langues tchadiques (haoussa) avec le BOCHIMAN. Les théories différentes qui ont été avancées dans les études de le classification des langues africaines sont présentées chez M.Cohen 1947,24,9.1, Cole, 1971, Schachter,1971;pour l'égyptien seulement v. Hodge,1970, Polotsky,1964, Vycichl,1966, Korostovcev,1963,15 ss.

C'est dans une perspective plus large que H.G.Mukarovsky (1963,1964,1966a,1966b,1966c,1966-7, 1969a,1969b,1971,1972) met les langues chamito-sémitiques en relation avec les LANGUES AFRICAINES ET LE BASQUE. Il faut noter aussi l'étude de J.Zavadovskij (1965) sur le problème du SUBSTRAT NOIR (*zindj*) en Afrique du nord.

2.1.2.3. Le chamito-sémitique et les langues du Sahara central

Restons dans le cadre indiqué par J.Tubiana et discutons les langues du Sahara central. Même ici on pourrait enrichir la bibliographie des études respectives à côté de celles-là citées chez J.Tubiana (surtout Cerulli,1961,v.aussi chez Tubiana,1970). Comme revue voir Petráček (1972a,1967,1970,1972b,Tucker-Bryan,1966,Bryan,1971 - sur le plan morphologique; pour la bibliographie voir Tucker-Bryan,1956,Greenberg,1971,dont la théorie joint ces langues au groupe nilo-saharien(1966).

La famille a été définie récemment par J.Lukas (1971-2, les classifications anciennes chez Petráček,1965,1975b) et approfondie dans les travaux de Tucker-Bryan (1956,1966), Tubiana (1960,1963,1968-9,Dossier-pour le zaghawa), Petráček (pour le berti 1966,1967,1968,1971,1972b, 1975b,1975c) et par Greenberg (1966,1971).

Il y a maintenant au moins quatre hypothèses sur les rapports des langues du Sahara central avec les autres familles, ou plutôt quatre indications sur la possibilité des rapports des langues en question:

(1) HYPOTHÈSE NILO-SAHARIENNE proposée par Greenberg (1966,130 ss.) dans laquelle ces langues figurent aussi à côté du maba (de la branche maban de Greenberg). Les arguments sont tirés du vocabulaire et de la morphologie.

(2) HYPOTHÈSE CHAMITO-SÉMITIQUE proposée pour la dernière fois par Tubiana (1974) et fondée surtout sur les données de la phonologie historique et du vocabulaire. En égard au rapport supposé avec le maba, cette hypothèse a des affinités avec celle de Greenberg (No.1).

(3) Hypothèse de Tucker-Bryan (1966) qui indique quelques rapports des langues du Sahara central avec LES LANGUES DE L'AFRIQUE DU NORD-EST, surtout avec quelques langues couchitiques (en général dans les annotations p.171,173, bedauye 171,174, saho 172, bilin 188; ometo 199) ainsi au'avec d'autres langues (kunama 171,paranilotic 173,rashad-tegali-tagoi- 180, s. moru-ma-di, bongo, baghirmi, nilotique 183, nubien 188 et l'éthiopien 171). La plupart des rapprochements touchent alors les langues couchitiques et ils sont fondés exclusivement sur la morphologie. Les auteurs ne nient pas qu'ils sont surtout intéressés à la typologie.

(4) HYPOTHÈSE DE PETRÁČEK (1972,résumé de 1969 publié en 1974), qui ne pouvait pas confirmer les rapports indiqués par Cerulli (1961) entre les langues du Sahara central et le chamito-sémitique en général sur le plan phonologique, ce qui n'implique pas un état analogue (négatif) sur les autres plans (Petráček,1972,50; 1974,29). Elle admet aussi les rapprochements issus des contacts mutuels des langues du Sahara central avec les langues parlées par les pasteurs néolithiques du type anthropologique éthiopien (possiblement aussi par des populations qui parlaient les langues couchitiques ou protocouchitique, Petráček,1966,1958-68;1975a; voir aussi les hypothèses de J.Lukas,1963a,1963b,1963c,1937,1939 etc.). Cette hypothèse n'exclut pas certains rapprochements possibles pour les branches africaines du chamito-sémitique (couchitique,tchadique) et les langues du Sahara central.

L'hypothèse déjà célèbre de L.Reinisch (1873) fondée sur le téda doit rester en dehors de notre classification bien qu'elle apporte de riches matériaux dont l'interprétation est sans doute fausse.

La situation dans les études citées plus haut se présente ainsi:

NILO-SAHARIEN   SAHARIEN CENTRAL   CHAMITO-SÉMITIQUE
                                                                  (COUCHITIQUE)

Greenberg
←————————————————————————————————————
plan lexical, morphologique

Tubiana   Cerulli, Tubiana
←————————————————————————————————————   ————————————————————————————————————→
plan lexical, maba   plan lexical, phonologique

                                         Tucker-Bryan
                                         ————————————————————————————————————→
                                         plan morphologique

                                         Petráček
                                         ————————————————————————————————————→
                                         plan phonologique négativement,
                                         chamito-sémitique en général

                                         Petráček, 1972, 49
                                         ————————————————————————————————————→
                                         plan phonologique couchitique -

                                         positivement pour la rétroflexive ḍ, avec la
                                         même possibilité pour le ton distinctif;

                                         Petráček, 1966, 1975a
                                         ————————————————————————————————————→
                                         plan morphologique, les coïncidences issues des
                                         contacts mutuels (affinité)

(AUTRES GROUPES)

Tucker-Bryan pour le
plan morphologique

Cette situation reflète un modèle de la situation dans la science linguistique qu'on ne
peut pas identifier avec la réalité linguistique du terrain en question. On en peut conclure
seulement la position de notre science.

Nous sommes, comme on le voit, portés à chercher des rapports de notre terme central (langues
du Sahara central) plutôt dans la direction de l'est, surtout avec les langues couchitiques
ou avec le chamito-sémitique africain. J.H. Greenberg pense plutôt aux rapports passant à
l'ouest ou au sud-ouest et el est suivi dans le cas de baba par J.Tubiana. Greenberg n'exclut
pas de rapports allant à l'est (nubien et les autres branches du nilo-saharien à l'Est
africain).

La méthodologie utilisée par nos confrères est différente. Des rapprochements lexicaux d'un
côté (Cerulli,Tubiana,Greenberg), la typologie morphologique de l'autre côté (Tucker-Bryan),
la reconstruction des systèmes ou de ses secteurs d'un caractère typologique (Petráček) et
l'application des contacts servant à expliquer les affinités sur le plan morphologique
(Petráček; à ajouter sont des hypothèses de Lukas basées sur l'anthropologie).

2.1.2.4. Problèmes de la méthode

Il n'est pas nécessaire de s'inquiéter de cette situation en exigeant l'application d'une
seule méthode, c'est-à-dire historique comparative. Nous savons que le caractère du groupe
chamito-sémitique n'est pas assez clair et on en dresse au moins deux modèles pour l'expliquer: l'un historique et génétique, l'autre aussi historique mais du caractère d'une
diffusion[3] [Pisani,1949,Garbini,1965,1972,1974, Fronzaroli,1971; discussion Petráček,1975a;
pour le sémitique Hetzron,1970,Rabin,1963,Grundfest,1969-1974,SSL 1973;177; la crise de la
théorie de l'arbre génétique est constatée par D.Cohen,1973;153; voir aussi le problème
des unions des langues et celui des affinités par contact, p.ex. dans le domaine éthiopien,
la riche littérature chez Zaborski,1975].

Même les érudits les plus célèbres de notre discipline conseillent à combiner l'étude des
plans de la langue à côté du plan traditionnel du comparativisme moderne qui sait apprécier
les plans différents (Katečić,1970,Serebrennikov,1973) ainsi que les méthodes de comparaison
différentes (Serebrennikov,1973) et la combinaison des dimensions diachronique et synchronique
(Trnka,1929). Bien sûr, il faut connaître précisément les limites d'une telle ou telle
méthode (pour la typologie dans nos études voir Petráček,1974b). La linguistique moderne
(Kuryłowicz,1964 et le problème de la reconstructions interne) autant que les tâches du
comparativisme sont changées.

Dans ce sens, l'opinion de J.Tubiana (1974;79) est circonspecte quand il exige que tout
rapprochement pûrement typologique doit être reservé, jusqu'à ce qu'on ait pu l'insérer
dans un tableau diachronique, car l'étude de la famille chamito-sémitique ne peut être qu'une
étude diachronique.

Ce sont les faits et les opinions bien connus, mais on peut discuter au moins deux questions:
le caractère de la parenté des langues chamito-sémitiques n'est pas clair et on peut admettre non seulement une famille mais aussi une union des langues (Sprachbund,v.plus haut).

Puis, il faut admettre la nécessité de compléter les investigations du plan phonologique et
des correspondances phonologiques par d'autres plans. Ou trouve une pleine et vaste discussion
(fondée sur une riche littérature) chez Katečić (1970,surtout ch.7 "Genetic Classification of
Languages"):

"Sound laws can therefore be used as the basic criterion for the genetic classification of languages as entities. This criterion, however, leads to a neat
classification only of those phonemic strings to which the sound laws in question
actually apply. Since all the phonemic strings of real languages never can be
derived by a single set of sound laws from the phonemic string of only one language,
it is always impossible to classify a language genetically just by stating the sound
laws by which its phonemic strings are derived from those of another (120) ....
The classification of whole languages, however, calls for additional criteria and
cannot be done on the basis of sound laws alone, since this criterion does not
lead to neat and unambiguous results (121) .... In other words, the language as a
whole must be classified before we can know what is inherited and what is borrowed"
(121).

Il est inutile d'entrer dans les détails de ce problème compliqué de la méthode comparative.
Tout montre qu'il est raisonnable, même dans la situation du chamito-sémitique, de combiner
les méthodes d'investigation. Pour le chamito-sémitique voir maintenant la discussion chez
Petráček (1975,sous presse,ch. "Les perspectives du comparativisme chamito-sémitique").

2.1.2.5. Problèmes à resoudre

C'est avec raison que J.Tubiana invite nos confrères à la recherche d'un phonème CACUMINAL *ḍ*
en chamito-sémitique (91 sq.) et pense à l'interprétation du *ḍāḍ* arabe (*ḍ* latéralisé d'après
J.Cantineau) comme un *ḍ* cacuminal (91), ce qui tisserait un lien de plus entre le sémitique
et le couchitique. La même hypothèse est exprimée dans mon étude (Petráček,1972;25): "Die
komplizierte Problematik des lateralen oder lateralisierten *d* in der Reihe der semitischen
emphatischen Laute könnte vielleicht an eine kuschitische Retroflexive hinweisen." Ce
problème est indiqué comme un éventuel point de contact entre les langues du Sahara central et
le chamito-sémitique: "In diesem einzigen Glied könnte ein Berührungspunkt mit dem semito-
hamitischen System verborgen sein, besonders mit den Systemen einiger kuschitischen
Sprachen ...." (49).

Mes opinions sont encadrées dans une hypothèse d'épanouissement de la corrélation du travail
accessoire dans les langues sémitiques et chamito-sémitiques. Comme le montre aussi la discussion chez Tubiana (1974) et mes projets (1972a), il semble que le temps soit venu pour
dresser une nouvelle théorie des "emphatiques" en chamito-sémitique.

La question des TONS DISTINCTIFS en deux branches africaines du chamito-sémitique (couchitique,
tchadique) est discutée en rapport avec les langues du Sahara central (94sq.) et elle a été
déjà caractérisée dans mon étude (Petráček,1972b;49): "Die prosodischen Eigenschaften der
zentralsaharanischen Sprachen werden durch die Ausnützung des Tones sehr markant charakter-
isiert, was für das semitohamitische System als Ganzes nicht bewiesen werden kann, auch wenn
hier in zwei afrikanischen Zweigen (im Tchadohamitischen und im Kuschitischen) ihre phono-
logische Relevanz ein älteres einheitliches System nicht ausschließen kann." Contre l'argumentation qu'il ne s'agit que d'un trait ancien, il faut souligner que certains travaux
montrent (ou supposent) le caractère secondaire du système des tons dans les langues du
Sahara central (Cyffer,1971 pour le kanuri) et en tchadique (Jungraithmayr,1974,3.3).

L'étude comparée du lexique visant la constance des correspondances phonologiques met de
nouveau en relief les possibilités du rapprochement surtout des langues du Sahara central et
des langues couchitiques. L'initiative de E.Cerulli (1961) dans ce problème est d'un grand
mérite ainsi que la continuation dans les études de J.Tubiana, dont la dernière (1974) résume
les autres travaux de l'auteur. J.Tubiana caractérise avec circonspection ces rapprochements comme "singulières coïncidences" (98).

Pour tirer de ces rapprochements de E.Cerulli et J.Tubiana des données utilisables au comparativisme génétique, il faudra dresser des PROTOSYSTÈMES des langues couchitiques et
sahariennes. Cette thèse est aujourd'hui valable même dans les études chamito-sémitiques et

africaines (surtout W. von Soden,1965,Dalby,1966 etc.). Nous savons quelle situation
chaotique règne dans les langues couchitiques où une telle reconstruction est difficile à
être faite sans une définition nouvelle de tout le groupe. Pour les langues du Sahara
central, nous avons à la disposition mes études (1967,1972a,b) d'un caractère synchronique,
pouvant (d'après J.H. Greenberg,1971,437) être utilisées pour les prochaines études diachron-
iques. Pour une telle étude diachronique, nous avons déjà quelques points de départ dans les
travaux de J.Lukas (1935), dans ceux de J.Tubiana ainsi que dans mes études sur le berti
(surtout les correspondances phonologiques entre berti et zaghawa dans mon étude "Berti and
the Central Saharan Group," 1975b, sous presse). La reconstruction d'un protosystème phonologique des langues du Sahara central est une question urgente. Le même vaut pour le
couchitique, où la situation est encore compliquée, mais favorable, grâce aux travaux de
départ de Dolgopolskij (1966,1973 etc.) et des autres (Illič-Svityč,1971;Zaborski,1970; la
situation en général chez Zaborski,1975).

Pour compléter le tableau des coïncidences et rapprochements aussi dans les autres plans
outre le plan phonologique, il faudra faire le même dans le plan morphologique, c'est-à-dire
faire la reconstruction des protoformes dans les deux groupes comparés. D'après mes recherches
préliminaires, il me semble que les points de départ les plus prometteurs pour l'étude comparative entre les langues chamito-sémitiques et les langues du Sahara central sont les
suivantes:

LE SYSTÈME VERBAL où nous avons à la disposition les analyses assez développées pour le
chamito-sémitique (pour le couchitique,v.le travail de Zaborski,1974 sous presse; à côté des
synthèses classiques, le tableau chez Tucker-Bryan,1968) et pour les langues du Sahara
central (Tucker-Bryan,1966, Bryan,1971, Lukas,1951-2).

LE SYSTÈME PRONOMINAL, surtout les études de Tucker (1967) pour le chamito-sémitique, à côté
des études anciennes de Reinisch (1909) et de Castellino (1962); pour les langues du Sahara
central Tucker-Bryan,1966, d'autres matériaux chez Bryan,1968.

LE NOM, ses catégories et ses formes sont aussi à poursuivre.

2.1.2.6.1. LES AUTRES RAPPROCHEMENTS DES LANGUES DU SAHARA CENTRAL

Il est nécessaire de suivre aussi les rapports des langues du Sahara avec les langues TCHADIQUES
(Greenberg,1960, Prietze,1908, Schubert,1972, Tubiana,1970) et surtout de repenser l'hypothèse "TCHADOHAMITIQUE" projetée dans les travaux de J.Lukas (1936a,1936b,1936c,1937,1939
etc.), reprise par D.Westermann et M.A.Bryan (1952), laquelle a joué un rôle important dans
la linguistique africaine mais qui paraît être reconstruite ou rejetée aujourd'hui (Newman,
1974, Terry,1971).

La question de la parenté du HAOUSSA a entre autre trouvé une issue spécial dans la thèse de
Parsons (1970) niant les rapports du haoussa avec le tchadique et visant aux rapports avec
UNE LANGUE SAHARIENNE qui pourrait être proche à l'égyptien et par là au chamito-sémitique.

2.1.2.6.2. LES LANGUES DU SAHARA CENTRAL ET LE NILO-SAHARIEN (FUR, MABA)

Il semble utile attirer l'attention sur les rapprochements entre les langues du Sahara central
et les braches du nilo-saharien (Greenberg,1966,1971). Cette famille attend encore sa définition approfondie et sa vérification. En tout cas, certains rapprochements entre ces langues
ont été signalés dans le plan morphologique (Greenberg, 1966,130-33) à côté des rapprochements
lexicaux (voir aussi Tubiana,1974).

Voici les rapports entre les langues du Sahara central et les autres branches du nilo-
saharien (1.songhai, 2.maban, 3.fur, 5.chari-nile, 6.coman) d'après les données chez Greenberg
paraissent comme il suit:

INDEX DE BRANCHES EN RELATION	N^OS. DES FAITS LINGUISTIQUES
1 2 3 4 5 6	1
1 2 3 4 5	2
2 3 4 5	37
1 2 6	12
1 2	8
2 3	19,24
2 4	6,46
2 5	38,40

Les langues du Sahara central sont le plus souvent rapprochées du songhai (1-4 fois), maban (3-4) fois, fur (4-4 fois) et du groupe chari-nile (5-4 fois). Sour chari-nile se cache un large groupe de langues, tandis que le fur est une langue unique et le maban un petit groupe de 4 membres seulement. Il en suit que les rapprochements les plus forts au point de vue quantitatif sont ceux qui lient les langues du Sahara central avec le FUR et le MABAN. Pour poursuivre les recherches dans la direction du fur, nous sommes dans une favorable situation grâce à la publication de la grammaire par A.C.Beaton (1968) à côté de Tucker-Bryan (1966, 219 sq.) qui indiquent aussi les rapprochements entre maba (220,221,224) et les autres langues.

Quant au fur et au maba, il y a quelques coïncidences que j'ai notées pendant mes études sur le berti qui appartient aussi au groupe de langues du Sahara central (Petráček,1975b, 1975c) et se rapproche surtout du zaghawa.

Le suffix du pluriel des noms en berti (-*to*/*tu* etc.) a ses reflets dans les langues du Sahara central (Petráček,1968) mais aussi dans une forme accentuée dans le maba (Tucker-Bryan,1966: 198; un exemple chez Tubiana,1974,101 *momok*,pl. *momok-otu*). F.Müller (1877:179) présente un exemple qui pourrait expliquer le mon des Berti, qui s'appellent eux-mêmes seulement *Siga-to*. Le nom "*berti*" doit signifier (Arkell,1961,179,Spence,1917,v.Petráček,1975c) "les esclaves." Il n'est pas exclu que le nom soit d'origine berti (*mir*-'esclave', nou savons que berti m- correspond à *b*- dans les autres langues du Sahara central, surtout en zaghawa, Petráčik,1975c: 'étoile': berti *mar*, zaghawa *bar* etc). Mais i'analogie avec le maba est frappante: du singulatif *bor-ik* ('esclave') le pluriel est formé par le suffixe -*tū*, *bor-tū* (v. Müller,1977,179).

Dans le fur, j'ai pu constater la coïncidence de la particule négative dans le verbe -*ba* en fur et en berti. Cette particule est aussi enregistrée dans les langues couchitiques et inter- prêtée par Dolgopolskij (1973,39) et par Zaborski (1974,150,190 ms.). Elle se trouve aussi dans d'autres langues du Soudan (daju etc.).

Les rapprochements lexicaux entre le berti et le fur ne sont pas sans intérêt, même quand il s'agit quelques fois de mots itinérants ('cheval': berti *burto*, fur *murta*, voir Mac Michael, 1920, 1922,I,119, n. 2, Tubiana,1960, 1970 pour les langues du Sahara central). Mais voir aussi:

FUR		BERTI
iya	'mère'	*iyo*
nina	'viande'	*ni, nito* etc.

Les recherches sont à pursuivre.

Pour le nom *iya* ('mère') nous pouvons constater aussi d'autres analogies (en nandi, suk) et
surtout en nubien (midob:*iyo*;kenuz,*dair*). Ceci nous amène à poser la dernière question, celle
des rapports entre les langues du Sahara central et la langue *nubienne*. Les coïncidences
entre le téda et le nubien furent déjà constatées par Reinisch (1873,406-7 pour la structure
verbale; Zyhlarz,1928 pour le kanuri). Nous savons que les Midob sont les voisins les plus
proches des Berti (la situation est décrite dans Mac Michael,1912), on pourrait alors
penser plutôt aux affinités dans le lexique (Mac Michael,1918,en général Zyhlarz,1928) mais
parfois il s'agit des noms du lexique de base:

MIDOB		BERTI
al	'bouche'	*a*
iya	'mère'	*iyo*
urri	'nom'	*tirr* etc.

Ici les études sont aussi à poursuivre.

D'autre part on peut voir les rapprochements entre le nubien et le couchitique (Reinisch,1911,
Armbruster,1970, discussion chez Zaborski,1975) et le berbère (Vycichl,1961).

Il semble probable que ces rapprochements pourraient trouver une explication adéquate dans
la conception des affinités linguistiques causées par les contacts mutuels.

2.1.3. LES LANGUES CHAMITO-SÉMITIQUES

2.1.3.1. Unité et diversité des langues chamito-sémitiques

Au point de vue méthodologique, il semble utile d'insister non seulement sur la conception d'une
UNITÉ chamito-sémitique, mais aussi à la DIVERSITÉ de ses branches. Il est clair que chaque
branche chamito-sémitique a sa propre histoire pleine de traits spécifiques dont les sources
se trouvent dans la diversité des milieux linguistiques et sociaux où se développe chaque
branche. Pour nous limiter seulement au continent africain, nous pouvons souligner des
facteurs differents régissant (entre outre) l'histoire de la branche ÉGYPTIENNE (la durée
du temps, le grade du développement économique, ethnique, social etc.), du BERBÈRE (problèmes
du superstrat arabe, expansion des nomades, contacts avec le monde méditérranéen—Carthage,
Rome etc.), du TCHADIQUE (les contacts avec les peuples du Soudan, régression des sites
anciens vers le sud sous la pression des conditions changeantes défavorables après le
néolithique etc.) et enfin l'histoire des langues COUCHITIQUES avec leurs contacts mutuels
dans le plan linguistique et social entre ces langues et les langues sémitiques (anciennes
et modernes).

2.1.3.2. Méthodes de la linguistique aréale et génétique

Il résulte de la situation indiquée plus haut quel rôle important peut jouer dans notre domaine
la linguistique aréale (géographique) avec ses méthodes et ses conceptions ("area," union
des langues, Sprachbund), et les études spéciales sur les contacts entre les langues apparentées
et non-apparentées (en général Serebrennikov,1973,120, Weinreich,1953; pour le chamito-
sémitique v.Petráček,1975a, sous presse, Zaborski,1975), à côté de la linguistique génétique
(v.ici 2.4) appliquée dans sa forme moderne qui embrasse non seulement le plan phonologique,
mais aussi dans une certaine mesure le plan morphologique.

2.1.3.3. Modèle graduel des relations

Dans notre cas où nous voulons suivre la diversité des langues chamito-sémitiques il semble
utile à appliquer les méthodes qui nous permettent de dresser un modèle graduel des relations

entre les branches du chamito-sémitique, ou le chamito-sémitique et les autres langues. Il s'agit ici d'utiliser les conceptions des linguistes (Sapir,Swadesh,1960,1984,1971 etc., Voegelin,1974) et des sémitisants (Murtonen,1969, 1974, Bender,1971, 1974, 1975 et d'autres) ainsi que des africanistes qui travaillent avec les concepts hiérarchisés des "phyla."

2.1.3.4. Théorie générale et spéciale du chamito-sémitique

Pour le moment où nous en sommes, il me semble utile á quitter la conception générale de l'unité chamito-sémitique dans les études comparatives qui cherchent à établir les rapports entre le chamito-sémitique et les autres langues de l'Afrique. L'invitation à RECONSTRUIRE LES PROTO-SYSTÈMES partiaux pour chaque branche doit se faire sentir même ici. Bien que nous acceptions la solution donnée par des hypothèses des migrations ou de la diffusion qui veulent expliquer l'unité chamito-sémitique, cette invitation ne perd pas   son importance.

Pour la comparaison du chamito-sémitique avec les autres langues de l'Afrique il faut insister sur la division du chamito-sémitique en deux zones géographiques: asiatique (sémitique) et africaine (égyptien,couchitique,berbère,tchadique) avec certaines zones intermédiares de contacts (surtout en Éthiopie). Leur unité est garantie par la théorie GÉNÉRALE du chamito-sémitique, leur diversité exige une théorie SPÉCIALE. Ces deux théories sont d'ordre différent. Notre problème — les rapports entre les langues appartenant au chamito-sémitique et les langues africaines — appartient sans doute au cadre de la théorie SPÈCIALE. Les "diffusion-istes" et les "migrationistes" peuvent accepter cette thèse: les uns que les autres supposent la même chose vue d'un autre côté, c'est-à-dire l'influence du protosémitique (superstrat) aux langues africaines et leurs sémitisation (les "diffusionistes"), ou l'influence du sub-strat (adstrat) africain aux langues chamito-sémitiques apportées par les immigrants asiatiques (les "migrationistes").

On voit clairement que sans une théorie spéciale expliquant la diversité du chamito-sémitique on ne peut réussir dans la théorie générale, parce que la dernière est spécifiée par la théorie spéciale et sans cette spécification elle resterait sur une théorie vague et statique, tandis que dans le deuxième cas elle reçoit les traits dynamiques et se change en une théorie dynamique capable d'expliquer mieux les procédés riches et pleins de lois et de hasards historiques des langues chamito-sémitiques.

2.1.3.5. Vers une solution complexe

Les problèmes linguistiques dans cette partie de l'Afrique qui nous intéresse, c'est à dire au Soudan et en Afrique du Nord-Est où sont parlées les langues sans filiation apparente (comme le fur, le méroïtique) de même que les petites familles de langues (maban), sont compliqués. Ceci résulte sans doute d'un développement compliqué et dynamique de cette région dans les temps préhistoriques et historiques. Leur solution doit être aussi complexe. Nous sommes alors heureux de voir la vive activité des équipes qui travaillent dans la République du Soudan et dans les confins du Tchad dont les résultats comme ceux-là publiés ou annoncés par J.Tubiana (avec M.-J.Tubiana et d'autres,v.Dossier); par les élèves de J.Lukas et par lui-même, ainsi que par les savants participant au projet Djebel Marra et aux problèmes linguistiques du Soudan, aident à former une base solide des recherches futures. Des études accélérées dans le domaine tchadique et couchitique nous aident aussi à éclaircir les zones limitrophes du chamito-sémitique africain, qui sont d'importance primordiale pour avancer dans la solution des problèmes des relations entre les langues chamito-sémitiques et les langues africaines. De cette solution dépend aussi la position du chamito-sémitique dans les modèles des relations des langues du monde.

2.1.4. BIBLIOGRAPHIE

Adams, G.B.,   1970   "Hamito-Semitic and the Pre-Celtic Substratum in Ireland and Britain," *Colloquium on Hamito-Semitic Comparative linguistics*, London, preprint (now: Th. & J.Bynon, eds. *Hamito-Semitica*, The Hague: Mouton, 1975)

Arkell, A.J.,   1961   *A History of the Sudan. From the Earliest Times to '82',* London

Armbruster, C.A.,   1960   *Dongolese Nubian. A Grammar,* Cambridge

Beaton, A.C.,   1968   *A Grammar of the Fur Language.* University of Khartoum. Linguistic Monograph Series Nr.1, M

Bender, M.L.,   1966   "Analysis of a Barya Word List," *Anthropological Linguistics*, 1-24

     1971   "The Languages of Ethiopia. A New Lexicostatistic Classification and Some Problems of Diffusion," *Anthropological Linguistics* 13, 165-288

     1972   "Linguistic Indeterminancy or Why You Cannot Reconstruct 'Proto-Human'," preprint

     1973   *Omotic. A New Afroasiatic Language Family,* preprint, now (1975) published by the University Museum of the Southern Illinois University, Carbondale, Illinois

     1974   "Consonant Co-Occurrence Restrictions in Afroasiatic Verb-Roots," preprint, Second Int. Congress on Hamito-Semitic Linguistics, Firenze

Brunner, L.,   1969   *Die gemeinsamen Wurzeln des semitischen und indogermanischen Wortschatzes. Versuch einer Etymologie,* Bonn

Bryan, M.A.,   1968   "The *N/*K Languages in Africa," JAL 7, 169-217

     1971   "The Verb Classes in the East Saharan Languages." *Afrikanische Sprachen und Kulturen — Ein Querschnitt,* Hamburg, 224-234

Bryan, M.A., Tucker, A.N.,   1948   *Distribution of the Nilotic and Nilo-Hamitic Languages of Africa,* Oxford

Castellino, G.R.,   1962   *The Akkadian Personal and Verbal System in the Light of Semitic and Hamitic,* Leyden

Cerulli, E.,   1961   "Etiopico," in *Linguistica Semitica, Presente e Futuro,* Roma, 148-151

Cohen, D.,   1973   "La lexicographie comparée," in *Studies on Semitic Lexicography,* ed. by P. Fronzaroli, ed. Firenze 183-208

Cohen, M.,   1933-   "Les résultats acquis de la grammaire comparée chamito-
     1955   sémitique," *Conférences de l'Institut de linguistique de l'Université de Paris, 1933 — Cinquante Années de recherches linguistiques, ethnographiques, critiques et pédagogiques,* 1955, 181 ss.

     1947   *Essai comparatif sur le vocabulaire et la phonétique du chamito-sémitique,* Paris

     1951   "Langues chamito-sémitiques et linguistique historique," *Scientia* 45, 177-9

Cole, D.T.,   1971   "The History of African Linguistics to 1945," in the
                                       Th.A. Sebeok, ed., *Current Trends in Linguistics* 7,
                                       Linguistics in Sub-Saharan Africa, 1-27, The Hague

Cuny, A.,   1924   *Études prégrammaticales*, Paris

                               1930   *La catégorie de duel dans les langues indo-européennes
                                       et chamito-sémitiques*, Brussel

                               1935-   "La famille linguistique indoeuropéenne considérée
                               1938   dans les rapports avec le groupe chamito-sémitique,"
                                       MIFAO 66, 257-66

                               1943   *Recherches sur le vocabulaire, le consonantisme et
                                       la phonétique des racines en nostratique*, Paris

                               1946   *Invitation à l'étude comparative des langues indo-
                                       européennes et langues chamito-sémitiques*, Bordeaux

Cyffer, N.,   1971   "Versuch einer Beschreibung der tonalen Verhältnisse
                                       im Kanuri von Maiduguri," *Afrikanische Sprachen und
                                       Kulturen — ein Querschnitt*, Hamburg, 235-245

Delitzsch, F.,   1873   *Studien über indogermanisch-semitische Wurzelverwand-
                                       schaft*, Leipzig

Dolgopolskij, B.A.,   1964   "Gipoteza drevnejšego rodstva jazykovyx semej
                                       severnoj Evrazii s verojatnostnoj točki zrenija,"
                                       Voprosy jazykonanija 2, 53-63

                               1966   "Materialy po sravniteljno-istoričeskoj fonetike
                                       kušitskix jazykov: gubnyje i dentaljnyje smyčnyje v
                                       načaljnom položenii," *Jazyki Afriki, Voprosy kultury,
                                       istorii i tipologii*, Moskva, 35-88

                               1968   "Metody rekonstrukcii obšče indoevropejskogo jazyka
                                       i vneindoevropejskije sopostavljenija," *Problemy
                                       sravniteljnoj gramatiki indoevropejskix jazykov*,
                                       Moskva

                               1971   "Nostratičeskye etimologii i proizxoždenye glagolnych
                                       formantov," *Etimologija* 1968, (1971), 227-243

                               1973   *Sravniteljno-istoričeskaya fonetika kušitskix jazykov*,
                                       Moskva

Dossiers de la R.C.P. n° 45   *Populations anciennes et actuelles des confins Tchado-
                                       Soudanais*, Paris

Drexel, A.,   1924   "Der semitische Triliteralismus und die afrikanische
                                       Sprachforschung," WZKM 31, 1924, 219-36; 32, 1925, 1-30.

Ehret, C.,   1971   *Southern Nilotic History-Linguistic Approach to the
                                       Study of the Past*, Evanston

                               1974   *Ethiopians and West-Africans: the Problem of Contacts*,
                                       Nairobi (sous presse)

Fraenkel, M.,   1970   *Zur Theorie der Lamed-He Stämme. Gleichzeitig ein
                                       Beitrag zur semitisch-indogermanischen Sprachwissen-
                                       schaft*

Fronzaroli, P.,   1973   "Statistical Methods in the Study of Ancient Near
                                       Eastern Languages," *Orientalia* 44, 77-118

                               1974   "Réflexions sur la paléontologie linguistique," *Actes
                                       du premier Congrès Int. de linguistique sémitique et
                                       chamitosémitique*, Paris 16-19 juillet 1969, 173-80

Gabelentz, G.v.d.,	1893	*Baskisch und Berberisch*, Berlin
Garbini, G.	1965	"La semitistica: definizione e prospettive di una disciplina," *AION* 15, 1-15, 1972
	1972	*Le lingue semitiche. Studi di storia linguistica*, Napoli
	1974	"L'egiziano e le lingue semitiche," preprint. Second Int. Congress on Hamito-Semitic Linguistics, Firenze
Gelb, I.,	1969	*Sequential Reconstruction of Proto-Akkadian*, Chicago
Ginneken, J.van,	1938	*L'importance des latérales caucasiennes pour l'étude des langues africaines, indoeuropéennes et chamito-sémitiques, Contribution à la grammaire comparée des langues du Caucase*
	1939a	*Reconstruction typologique des langues archaïques de l'humanité,*
	1939b	"Ein neuer Versuch zur Typologie der älteren Sprach-strukturen," *TCLP* 8, 233-261
Goodman, M.,	1971	"The Strange Case of Mbugu," in *Pidginization and Creolization of Languages*, ed., D.Hymes, Cambridge, 243-254
Greenberg, J.H.,	1957	"'Nilotic', 'Nilo-Hamitic' and Hamito-Semitic. A Reply," *Africa* 27, 364-378
	1960	"Linguistic Evidence for the Influence of the Kanuri on the Hausa," *JAH* 1,205-12
	1966	*Languages of Africa*, 2.ed., The Hague
	1971	"Nilo-Saharan and Meroitic," in Th.A. Sebeok, ed., *Current Trends in Linguistics, 7, Linguistics in Sub-Saharan Africa*, The Hague, 421-442
Grundfest, Y.D.,	1974	"The Problem of Classifying Southern Semitic Languages," *IV. Congresso internazionale di studi etiopici*, Roma, t.II, sezione linguistica, Roma, 105-114, aussi Moscou en forme d'un tiré à part
Haldar, H.,	1966	*Language and Culture*, New York
Harris, Z.S.,	1944	"Yocuts Structure and Newman's Grammar," *IJAL* 196-211 — *Papers in Structural and Transformational Linguistics*, Dordrecht 1970
Heilmann, L.,	1949	*Camito-semitico e indoeuropeo*, Bologna
Hetzron, R.,	1970	"The Classification of Ethiopian Semitic," preprint, Colloquium on Hamito-Semitic Comparative Linguistics, London (now (1975) in J. and Th. Byron, eds., *Hamito-Semitica*, The Hague)
Hodge, C.T.	1970	"Afroasiatic. An Overview," in Th.A. Sebeok ed., *Current Trends in Linguistics, 6, Linguistics in South West Asia and North Africa*, 237-254, The Hague
Hohenberg, J.,	1956	"Comparative Masai Word List," *Africa* 26, 281-89
	1958a	"Some Notes on Nilotic, 'Nilo-Hamitic' by J.H. Green-berg," *Africa* 28, 37-42
	1958b	*Semitisches und hamitisches Sprachgut in Masai mit vergleichendem Wörterbuch*

Homburger, L., 1928 "Les noms égyptiens des parties du corps dans les langues négro-africaines," *Comptes rendus de l'Ac. des Inscriptions*, 28 déc. 1928

1939 *Études de linguistique négro-africaine 1. Les formes verbales*, Chartres

1949a *The Negro-African Languages*, London

1949b "Les dravidiens en Afrique," *Actes du XXIᵉ Congrès des orientalistes*, 1948,1949, 367-8

1954 "Éléments dravidiens en somali," *BSLP 50*, XXV

1955 "L'Inde et l'Égypte," *JA 243*, 129-30

1957 *Les langues négro-africaines et les peuples qui les parlant*, Paris 2ᵉᵐᵉ éd.

1960- "Sur l'origine de quelques langues couchitiques,"
1963 *GLECS 9*, 54-7

Honorat, M., 1933 *Démonstration de la parenté de la langue chinoise avec les langues japhétiques, sémitiques et chamitiques*, Paris

Huntingford, G.W.B. 1956 "The 'Nilo-Hamitic' Languages," *Southwestern Journal of Anthropology 12*, 200-22

Illič-Svityč, V.M. 1964 *Genesis indoevropeiskix rjadov gutturalnyx v svete dannyx vnešnogo sravnenija, Problemy sravniteljnoj gramatiki indoevropejskix jazykov, Tezisy dokladov*, Moskva

1967 "Materialy k sravniteljnomu slovaru nostratičeskix jazykov," *Etimologija 1965*, Moskva

1968 "Sootvestvija smyčnyx v nostratičeskix jazykov," *Etimologija 1966*, Moskva, 304-355

1971a "Ličnyje mestoimenija mi 'ja' i mǎ 'my' v nostratičes-kom," *Issledovanija po slavjanskom jazykoznaniju, Sbornik v čest'* ... S.B. Bernštejna, 396-406, Moskva

1971b "Opyt sravnenija nostratičeskix jazykov (semitoxamitskij, altajskij)." Vvendenkje. Sravniteljnyj slovar /b-Ķ/, Moskva

Isserlin, B.S.J., 1970 "Some Aspects of the Present State of Hamito-Semitic Studies," *Colloquium on Hamito-Semitic Linguistics*, London 1970, preprint

Jungraithmayr, H., 1974 "A Tentative Four Stage Model for the Development of the Tchadic Languages," *Second Int. Congress on Chamito-Semitic Linguistics*, Firenze, preprint

Katečič, R., 1970 *A Contribution to the General Theory of Comparative Linguistics*, The Hague

Kluge, Th., 1947 "Die Zahlenbegriffe (4) der Draviden, Hamiten, Semiten und Kaukasiern," c.r. in *Language 23*, 1947

Korostovcev, M.A., 1963 *Vvedenije v egipetskuju filologiju*, Moskva

Kuryłowicz, J., 1964 "On the Methods of Internal Reconstruction," *Proceedings of the Ninth Int. Congress of Linguists*, Cambridge, Mass., 1962, the Hague, 9-36

Łahovary, N.,   1963   *Dravidian Origins and the West. Newly Discovered Ties with the Ancient Cultures and Languages, incl. Basque, of the Pre-Indo-European Mediterranean World*

Leesberg, A.C.M.,   1905   *Comparative Philology. A Comparison Between Semitic and American Languages*

Leslau, W.   1961   c.r. Hohenberg, 1958, Language 37, 176-9

Levin, S.,   1971   *The Indo-European and Semitic Languages. An Exploration of Structural Similarities Related to Accent, Chiefly in Greek, Sanskrit and Hebrew*, Albany

Lukas, J.,   1935   "Lautlehre des Bādawi-Kanuri in Borno," *ZfES* 25, 1934, Berlin 1935, 3-29

     1936a   "Hamitisches Sprachgut im Sudan," *ZDMG* 90, 579-88

     1936b   "The Linguistic Situation in the Lake Chad Area in Central Africa," *Africa* 1936, 332-49

     1936c   "Uber den Einfluss der hellhäutigen Hamiten auf die Sprachen des zentralen Sudans," *Forschungen und Fortschritte* 12 /14/, 180-1

     1937   *Zentralsudanische Studien*, Hamburg

     1939   "Die Verbreitung der Hamiten in Afrika," *Scientia*, février 1939

     1951-   "Umrisse einer ostsaharischen Sprachgruppe," *Afrika*
     1952   *und Übersee* 36, 3-7

Mac Donald, C.,   1894   *Asiatic Origin of the Oceanic Languages: Etymological Dictionary of the Language Efate (New Hebrides)*, London

     1896   "The Asiatic or Semitic Origin of the Oceanian Numerals, Personal Pronouns, Phonology and Grammar," *J. of the Polynesian Society* 5, 212-232

     1889   *Oceania - Linguistics and Anthropological*, Melbourne-London

     1899   "Asiatic Relationship of Oceanic Languages," *J. of the Polynesian Society* 8, 197-203

     1901   "The Asiatic (Semitic) Relationship of the Oceanian Family of Languages: Triliteralism and Internal Vowel Change," *J. of the Polynesian Society* 13, 57-64

     1907   *The Oceanic Languages, Their Grammatical Structure, Vocabulary and Origin*, London-Edinbourgh

Mac Michael, H.A.,   1912   "Notes on the Zaghawi and the People of Gebel Midob, Anglo-Egyptian Sudan," *Journal of Anthropological Institute* 42, 288-348

     1920   "Darfur Linguistics," *SNR* 3, 197-216

     1922   A *History of the Arabs in the Sudan*, I,

     1928   "Nubian Elements in Darfur," *SNR* 1, 33-53

Marr, N.J.,   1886   *Osnovnyje tablicy k gramatike drevne-gruzinskogo jazyka s predjvariteljnym soobščenijem o rodstve gruzinskogo jazyka s semitičeskimi, v. aussi Iverin,* Tbilisi, 1886, no. 86

	1933	*Voprosy jazyka v osvěščenii jafetičeskoj teorii,* Leningrad
	1933- 1934	*Izbrannyje raboty,* Leningrad
Meeussen, A.E.	1957	"Hamitisch en Nilotisch," *Zaïre* 11, no.3, 263-72
Meinhof, C.,	1910	*Die moderne Sprachforschung in Afrika,* Berlin
	1911	"Das Ful in seiner Bedeutung für die Sprachen der Hamiten, Semiten und Bantu," *ZDMG* 65, 177-220
	1922a	*Die Sprachen der Hamiten,* Hamburg
	1922b	"Was können uns die Hamitischen Sprachen für den Bau des semitischen Verbums lehren?", *ZES* 12, 241-275
	1930	"Das Verhältnis der Buschmansprache zum Hottentotischen," *WZKM* 37, 219-229
Meriggi, P.,	1927	"Il problema della parantella dell'indoeuropeo con semitico," *Festschrift C. Meinhof,* Hamburg, 416-24
Meščaninov, I.I.,	1936	*Novoje učenije o jazyke,* Moskva
	1940	*Obščeje jazykoznanije,* Moskva
	1950	*Pražské přednášky o jazyce,* Praha
Moeller, H.,	1908	"Die gemein-idg.-semitischen Worttypen der zwei und drei konsonantigen Wurzeln in den idg.-semitischen vokalischen Entsprechungen," *Z. f. vergleichende Sprachforschung auf dem Gebiet der idg. Sprachen,* 42, 174-91
	1911	*Vergleichendes Indogermanisch-Semitisches Wörterbuch*
	1920	"Zur Vorgeschichte des idg. Genitivs sing.," *Z. f. vergleichende Sprachforschung auf dem Bebiet der idg. Sprachen,* 49, 219-29
	1917	*Die semitisch-vorindogermanischen laryngalen Konsonanten,* København
Moscati, S., Spitaler,A., Ullendorff, E., Soden, W. von,		
	1964	*An Introduction to the Comparative Grammar of the Semitic Languages.* Phonology and Morphology, Wiesbaden
Mukarovsky, H.G.,	1963	*Die Grundlagen des Ful und des Mauretanischen,* Wien
	1964	"Baskisch und Berberisch," *WZKM* 59/60, 52-94
	1966a	"Les rapports du basque et du berbère," *GLECS* 10, 177-84
	1966b	"Über den Grundwortschatz des Eurosaharanischen," *Mitteilungen zur Kulturkunde* 1 (≡ *Paideuma* 12), 135-149
	1966c	"West African and Hamito-Semitic Languages," *Wiener völkerkundliche Mitteilungen* 8, 9-36
	1966- 1967	"Langues apparentées au chamito-sémitique," *GLECS* 11, 83-91, 160-172
	1969a	"Baskisch-berberischen Entsprechungen," *WZKM* 62, 32-51

	1969b	"Über die Lautgesetzlichkeiten berberisch-baskischen Entsprechungen," *ZDMG*, Suppl. I.: XXVII. *Deutschen Orientalistentag* 1137-1143
	1971	"Die Zahlwörter 'eins' bis 'zehn' in den Mande-Sprachen," *Afrikanische Sprachen und Kulturen-ein Querschnitt*, 142-153
	1972	*El Vascuence y el Bereber, Euskera* (Bilbao), 17, 5-48
Müller, F.,	1877	*Grundriss der Sprachwissenschaft*, II. Bd., Wien
Murtonen, A.,	1969	*Early Semitic II. Lexico- and Phonostatistical Survey of the Structure of the Semitic Stock of Languages with Special Reference to South Semitic*, Melbourne
	1974	"Hebrew, Harari and Somali Statistically Compared," *Actes du premier Congrès int. de la linguistique sémitique et chamito-sémitique*, Paris 16-19 juillet 1969, The Hague, 68-75
Newman, P.,	1974	"Chado-Hamitic 'Adieu': New Thoughts on Chadic Classification," *Second Int. Congress on Hamito-Semitic Linguistics*, Firenze, preprint
O'Grady, G.N.,	1971	"Lexicographic Research in Aboriginal Australia," in Th.A. Sebeok ed., *Current Trends in Linguistics, 8, Linguistics in Oceania*, The Hague, 779-803
Palmer, F.R.,	1970	"Cushitic," in Th.A. Sebeok ed, *Current Trends in Linguistics, 6, Linguistics in South West Asia and North Africa*, The Hague, 571-85
Parsons, F.W.,	1970	"Prolegomena on the Status of Hausa," *Colloquium on Hamito-Semitic Linguistics*, London 1970, preprint
Pedersen, J.	1927	*Semiten, Reallexicon der Vorgeschichte*, s.v.
Petráček, K.,	1965	"Phonetik, Phonologie und Morphonologie der Berti-(Siga) Sprache in Dār Fūr (Sūdān)," *ArOr* 33, 341-66
	1966	"Jazyková situace v Africe," in I.Hrbek a kol., *Dějiny Afriky*, I, Praha, 150-68
	1967	"Phonologische Systeme der zentralsaharanischen Sprachen (konsonantische Phoneme)," *ArOr* 35, 26-51
	1968	"Morphologie (Nomen, Pronomen) der Berti-(Siga) Sprache in Dār Fūr (Sūdān)," *ArOr* 34, 295-319
	1971	"Die Zahlwörtersysteme der zentralsaharanischen Sprachen," *Afrikanische Sprachen und Kulturen — ein Querschnitt*, Hamburg 246-9
	1972a	"Die Grenzen des Semitohamitischen: Die zentralsaharanischen und semitohamitischen Sprachen in phonologischer Hinsicht," *ArOr* 40, 1972, 6-50
	1972b	"Phonologische Systeme der zentralsaharanischen Sprachen (vokalische Phoneme)," *Mélanges Marcel Cohen*, The Hague, 389-96
	1974	"À propos des limites du chamito-sémitique: Les systèmes phonologiques des langues chamito-sémitiques et des langues du Sahara central," *Actes du premier Congrès*

int. de linguistique sémitique et chamitosémigique, Paris 16-19 juillet, 1969, The Hague, 27-29

1974b "La typologie et la linguistique chamito-sémitique," *Second Congress on Hamito-Semitic Linguistics,* Firenze 1974, preprint

1975a *Úvod do srovnávaciho studi a semitohamitských jazyků,* Praha (skripta FF UK) [Introduction à l'étude comparative des langues chamito-sémitiques], sous presse

1975b "Berti and the Central Saharan Group," R.Thelwall ed., *Language in Sudan,* London, sous presse

1975c "Die sprachliche Stellung der Berti- (Siga) Sprache in Dār Fūr (Sūdān)," *African and Asian Studies* (Bratislava), 11, sous presse

Pisani, V.,   1949   "Indoeuropeo e camito-semitico," *AION* 3, 333-9 in *Saggi di linguistica storica,* Torino, 1959, 71-8

Porkorný, J.,   1951   "Sprachliche Beziehungen zwischen dem Alten Orient und den Britischen Inseln," *ArOr* 19, 268-70

Polák, V.,   1950   "L'état actuel des études linguistiques caucasiennes," *ArOr* 18, 383-407

Polotsky, H.,   1964   "Semitics," "Egyptian," in E.A. Speiser (ed.), *The World History of the Jewish People,* first ser., vol. 1 *At the Dawn of Civilisation,* Tel Aviv, 99-111, 121-123

Prietze, R.,   1908   "Die spezifischen Verstärkungsadverbien im Haussa und Kanuri," *MSOS* 11, *Afrikanische Studien*

Rabin, C.,   1963   "The Origin of the Subdivision of Semitic," *Hebrew and Semitic Studies Presented to G.H.Driver,* Oxford, 104-115

Reinisch, L.,   1873   *Der einheitliche Ursprung der Sprachen der alten Welt nachgewiesen durch Vergleichung der afrikanischen, erythräischen und indogermanischen Sprachen mit Zugrundelegung des Tuda,* Wien

                                 1911   *Die sprachliche Stellung des Nuba,* Wien

                                 1909   *Das persönliche Pronomen und Verbalflexion in den chamitosemitischen Sprachen,* Wien

Rössler, O., & Wagner, H.,   1960   "Das Verbum in den Sprachen der Britischen Inseln. Ein Beitrag zur geographischen Typologie," *Z. für Celtische Philologie,* 28, 142 ss.

RSO   *Rassegna delgi studi orientali,* Roma

Schachter, P.,   1971   "The Present State of African Linguistics," in Th.A. Sebeok ed., *Current Trends in Linguistics,* 7, *Linguistics in Africa,* 30-44, The Hague

Schenkel, W.,   1971   "Das altägyptische Pseudopartizip und das indogermanische Medium/Perfekt," *Orientalia* 40, 301-16

Schoot, A.,   1936   "Indogermanisch-Semitisch-Sumerisch, Germanen und Indogermanen," *Festschrift für H.Hirt,* 45-95, Heidelberg

Schröder, E.E.W.G.,   1929   *Über die semitischen und nicht-indischen Grundlagen der Malaisch-polynesischen Kultur,* Bd. II: *Das Verhältnis der austronesischen zu den semitischen Sprachen*

Schubert, K.,	1972	*Zur Bedeutung und Anwendung der Verbalparadigmen im Hausa und Kanuri*, Hamburg
Serebrennikov, V.A.,	1973	*Obščeje jazykoznanije. Metody lingvističeskix issledovanii*, Moskva
Skalička, V.,	1974	"Slovník nostratických jazyků," compte rendu de Illič-Svityč, 1971b, *Jazykovědné aktuality* 11, no. 1, 22-4
Soden, W. von,	1973	"Ein semitisches Wurzelwörterbuch. Probleme und Möglichkeiten," *Orientalia* 42, 142-148
Spence, B.H.H.,	1917	*Sagatu-ā. A Vocabulary of the Dialect of the Sagatu, or Berti Inhabitate of Northern Darfur*, Compiled ... March 1917, ms. Khartoum University, File No. 1294/4 O LOPR
SSL	1973	"South Arabian and Ethiopic Lexicography," in *Studies on Semitic Lexicography*, ed. P. Pronzaroli, 161-81
Stopa, R.,	1968	"Bushman Substratum or Bushman Origin in Hausa," *Folia Orientalia* 9, 151-234
	1972	*Structure of Bushman and its Traces in Indoeuropean*, Kraków
Swadesh, M.,	1960	"Tras la Huella Lingüistica de la Prehistoria," *Suplementos del Seminario de problemas scientificos y filosoficos*, No. 26, 2nd. ser., Mexico, Universidad Nacional de Mexico
	1964	"Linguistic Overview," in *Man in the New World*, ed. by J.D. Jennings, E.Norbeck, Chicago, 527-56
	1971	*The Origin and Diversification of Language*, Aldine-Atherton
Terry, R.R.,	1971	"Chadic," in Th.A. Sebeok ed., *Current Trends in Linguistics*, 7, *Linguistics in Sub-Saharan Africa*, The Hague, 443-454
Trnka, B.,	1929	"Méthode de comparaison analytique et grammaire comparée historique," *TCLP* 1, 33-38
Trombetti, A.,	1902-1903	"Delle relazioni delle lingue caucasiche con le lingue chamito-semitiche e con altri gruppi linguistici," *G. della Soc. Asiatica Italiana* 15, 1902, 177-201, 1903, 138-175
	1905	*L'Unità d'origine dell linguaggio*
	1923	*Elementi di glottologia*, Bologna
Tubiana, J.,	1954	"Sur la répartition géographique des dialectes agaw," *BSLP* 50, V-VII
	1968-1969	"Observations — À propos de sumór — 'lièvre' (toubou, tēda-daza)," *GLECS* 13, 84-6
	1959	"Note sur la distribution géographique des dialectes agaw," *Cahiers de l'Afrique et de l'Asie* 5, 297-306
	1960	"La mission du Centre National de la Recherche Scientifique aux confins du Tchad," *Cahiers d'études africaines* 1, 115-20
	1962	"À propos d'un dictionnaire mbay — français," *Journal de la Société des africanistes*, 32, 332-39

	1963	"Note sur la langue des Zaghawa," *Trudy XXV meždunarodogo kongressa vostokovedov*, t. 5, 614-619
	1968-1969	"Remarques sur le nom du liévre en teda, daza et dans les dialectes BêRî et en kulere," *GLECS* 13, 84-8
	1970	"Names of Animals and Plants in the Teda, Daza and BêRî Dialects," *Second Int. Conference* "Language and Literature in the Sudan," 7-12 Dec. 1970, Khartoum, pre-print
	1974	"Le chamito-sémitique et les langues africaines," *IV Congresso Int. di Studi Etiopici*, t.2, *Sezione linguistica*, Roma, 79-103
Tubiana, M.-J. et J.,	1961	*Contes Zaghawa*, Paris
	1968	*Field-Work in Darfour, I Ethnology, Linguistics, History*, Dossiers de la R.S.P. no. 45, 4, 1-16
Tucker, A.N.,	1967	"Fringe Cushitic: An Experiment in Typological Comparison," *BSOAS* 30, 655-80
Tucker, A.N., Bryan, M.A.,	1956	*The Non-Bantu Languages of North-Eastern Africa*, London
	1966	*Linguistic Analyses. The Non-Bantu Languages in North-Eastern Africa*, London
Voegelin, C.F. and F.M.,	1964	"Languages of the World: African Fascicle One," *Anthropological Linguistics* 6, Nr. 5
Vycichl, W.,	1961	"Berber Words in Nubian," *Kush* 9, 289-90
	1966	"Sprachliche Beziehungen awischen Ägypten und Afrika, Neue Afrikanische Studien" (*Hamburger Beiträge zur Afrika-Kunde*, Bd.5), 1966, 265-72
	1973	"Trois études sur la structure du Meroïtique," *Meroitic Newsletter* 13, 57-60
	1974	"Les études chamito-sémitiques à l'Université de Fribourg et le 'Lamékhite'", *Actes du Premier Congrès Int. de la linguistique sémitique et chamito-sémitique*, Paris 16-19 juillet 1969, The Hague, 60-67
Wagner, H.,	1959	*Das Verbum in den Sprachen der Britischen Inseln. Ein Beitrag zur geographischen Typologie des Verbums*, Tübingen
Weinreich, U.,	1953	*Languages in Contact*, New York
Westermann, D., Bryan, M.A.,	1952	*The Languages of West Africa*, London
Whiteley, W.W.,	1960	"Linguistic Hybrids," *African Studies* 19, 95-97
Zaborski, A.,	1970	"Materials for a Comparative Dictionary of Cushitic Languages: Somali:Galla Comparisons," *Colloquium on Hamito-Semitic Comparative Linguistics*, London, preprint
	1974	*Studies in Hamito-Semitic: The Verb in Cushitic*, sous presse
	1975	"Cushitic Overview"
Zavadovskij, Ju.N.,	1965	*Zindžskij substrat v severnoj Afrike, Semitskije jazyki*, 2 t., 1 p., 271-84, Moskva
Zyhlarz, E.,	1928	"Zur Stellung des Dārfūr Nubischen," *WZKM* 38, 84-123, 188-212

LE GRAPHE

TABLEAU

Indo-European	_8_	67 siècles		
Afro-Asiatic		_9_ 60	60	
Sudanese			_10_ 80	
Congolaise			_11_	67
Khoisan				_12_

3. SEMITICS

3.1. HAILU FULASS, "A pseudo-object construction in Amharic," in *IV Congresso Internazionale di Studi Etiopici (Roma, 10-15 aprile 1972)*, Tomo II, (Sezione Linguistica; Problemi Attuali di Scienza e di Cultura, 191). Rome: Accademia Nazionale dei Lincei, 1974, pp. 115-125.
By TALMY GIVÓN (University of California, Los Angeles)

This is a very lucid article, with well presented data that are easy to interpret, and a number of observations concerning the grammar of Amharic that are both interesting and, in some sense, intuitively 'right'. The main theme of the article revolves around the use of object suffix pronouns in an anaphoric construction such as:

(1) *leboččʼu yä-Mulu-n däbtäročč wässädu-bb-at*

    'thieves-the of-Mulu-Obj notebooks took-against-HER'
    'The thieves took Mulu's notebooks from her'

The author correctly notes that, unlike in other Amharic sentences where the object pronoun 'agrees' with a particular noun phrase that is actually present in the sentence (see further below), in this construction, much like in its translation in English, 'her' is an anaphoric pronoun, standing for the co-referential (and therefore deleted) noun phrase [from Mulu]. The 'deep structure' of a sentence such as (1) above is, presumably:

(2) **leboččʼu yä-Mulu-n däbtäročč Mulu-n wässädu*

    'thieves-the of-Mulu-Obj notebooks Mulu-Obj took'

where the first occurrence of Mulu is the genitive modifier of the accusative object 'notebooks', while the second occurrence is the one that becomes "pronominalized," i.e. the "dative" or "adversive" object (the indirect object of 'take away from'). The best proof for this is, of course, sentences such as (3) below, where the genitive modifier and the dative are NOT co-referential, and therefore the dative NP is not deleted. In either case, the dative/benefactive/adversive object controls the agreement of the pronoun:

(3) *lǝjoččʼu Kasa-n yä-Mulu-n däbtäročč wässädu-bb-ät*

    'children-the Kasa-Obj of-Mulu-Obj notebooks took-against-HIM'
    'The children took Mulu's notebooks from Kassa'

(4) **lǝjoččʼu Kasa-n yä-Mulu-n däbtäročč wässädu-bb-at*

    'children-the Kassa-Obj of-Mulu-Obj notebooks took-against HER'

In the course of the discussion, much data concerning the non-anaphoric use of object pronouns in Amharic is exposed, data which points in the direction of a highly universal process (see Talmy Givón, "Pronoun, Topic and Grammatical Agreement," presented at the CONFERENCE ON SUBJECT AND TOPIC, UCSB, March 8-9, 1975) by which pronominal systems develop into obligatory agreement systems. Roughly speaking, for accusative objects, agreement (or 'resumptive object pronoun') may not occur for indefinites, but may occur for definites:

(5) *le boččʼu däbtär wässädu*

    'thieves-the notebook took'
    'The thieves took away a book'

    le boččʼu däbtär-u-n wässädu-t

    'thieves-the notebook-THE-Obj took-IT'
    'The thieves took the notebook'

leboččǔ däbtär wässädu-t

The article further elaborates on data found in Haile (1970), to the effect that if both definite-accusative and (definite)-dative objects are present, the dative but not the accusative controls the pronoun agreement. The benefactive/adversive also takes precedence over the accusative in this regard. Thus, the hierarchy of grammatical agreement in Amharic conforms to universal hierarchies of the type:

(6) $\left\{\begin{array}{l}\text{dative}\\\text{benefactive}\\\text{adversive}\end{array}\right\}$ > def. accusative > accusative

With respect to the spread of grammatical agreement in Amharic, one may say that it has already spread from the dative/benefactive to the definite accusative, but not yet to the unrestricted accusative. Situations of this type are rather common intermediates in the spreading of grammatical agreement down the object-arguments paradigm (see Givón, o.c.). And the overall hierarchy involved is, basically, the hierarchy of DISCOURSE TOPICALITY, which may be more fully given as:

(7) subject > benefactive > dative > human accusative > def. accusative > accusative

Another interesting piece of data in this article concerns the shifting function of the definite object suffix -n. This suffix has been generalized to both the accusative, and dative/benefactive/adversive objects. So that when they are all definite, as in (3) above, this erstwhile case suffix has ceased to differentiate between the various semantic cases of objects. One may thus argue that the precedence of dative/benefactive/adversive object agreement over that of the accusative, even when both are definite, has by itself become a way of distinguishing non-accusative objects from accusatives in Amharic. Put another way, the object agreement phenomenon in Amharic may be spreading its function beyond the anaphoric, definitizer or topicalizer functions that are more predictable for such offshoots of the pronominal system (see details of those functions in Getatchew Haile (1970), "The Suffix Pronouns in Amharic," in Kim & Stahlke (eds.) *Papers in African Linguistics*, Edmonton: Ling. Research Inc.). One can also show that a similar situation may be developing in Spanish, where the erstwhile dative preposition *a* is spreading into HUMAN ACCUSATIVE objects, but datives overrule accusatives in object agreement, so that:

(8) *le-di el libro a Juan*   'I gave-HIM the book TO JOHN'

  *lo-di el libro a Juan   **'I gave-IT THE BOOK to John'

(9) *yo quiero a María*   'I love Mary'

  yo la-quiero   'I love her'

  ? yo la-quiero a María   'I love-HER MARY'   (OK only as emphatic)

  yo quiero un libro   'I want a book'

  *yo lo-quiero un libro

The author indulges, mostly in a number of lengthy footnotes, in highly abstract suggestions concerning the semantic analysis of verbs with more than one argument as expressions which involve "higher verbs." This suggestion, familiar to those who have followed Generative Semantics at least during its initial phases, is not really justified by syntactic data from Amharic, as distinct from semantic data from any other language. So that it neither adds to nor subtracts from the impact of the main topics discussed by the author. In a similar vein, the author's references to the pronominal prepositions -bb- and -ll- and their suppletive relation with the object definite suffix -n, again in a footnote, is not necessarily the most revealing way of viewing the situation, although somehow it does call attention to the growing interaction between the largely lost prepositions (which survive only in suffix-pronoun contexts), the rising object agreement and the object marker -*n*. Finally, an interesting problem of inalienable possession is brushed under the carpet rather quickly in fn. #4. On the whole, however, this is an extremely interesting article, and—for its slim size—a very welcome contribution.

3.2. GETATCHEW HAILE, "The copula ነው (näw) in Amharic," in *IV Congresso Internazionale di Studi Etiopici (Roma, 10-15 aprile 1972)*, Tomo II, (Sezione Linguistica; Problemi Attuali di Scienze e di Cultura, 191). Rome: Accademia Nazionale dei Lincei, 1974, pp. 139-154.
By M. LIONEL BENDER (Southern Illinois University, Carbondale, Illinois)

This article is, of course, not an attempt to tell all that is known about *nɛw*. Rather it concerns itself with one primary problem: "explaining" the fact that the copula takes the object pronominal suffixes rather than the subject suffixes. Getatchew concludes that the copula consists of a monoliteral verb *n* with the past-tense suffix -ɛ (as in the usual 3rd m. sg. verb, e.g. *t'ɛrrɛg-ɛ*, 'he swept') and the object pronominal suffixes agreeing with the surface subject (e.g. *mɛmhir nɛ-ň*, I am a teacher', *mɛmhir nɛ-š̌*, 'you (f.) are a teacher'). This analysis is well-motivated by analogy with the common impersonal verb construction, e.g. *rabɛ-ň*, 'I am hungry,' *rabɛ-š̌*, 'you (f.) are hungry').

There is nothing very new or startling about this analysis. However, two interesting etymological questions arise: what is the origin of the verb *n*, and the suffix (if indeed it is a suffix) -ɛ preceding the object suffixes?

As noted above, Getatchew argues that -ɛ is the past tense marker (p. 146). To make sense of the first paragraph on p. 156, I think we would have to reword it as ". . . the object pronominal suffixes, can be affixed to the verb or copula *n*. . ." (not "copula *näw*," as in the text). However, an alternative possibility is that the copula may be **nɛ*, incorporating the -ɛ. This would be parallel to the only other monoliteral verb in Amharic, *š̌a*, 'want, seek' (Dawkins 1969: 46). In fact, Dawkins says that *nɛw* is not a "true verb form," but consists of the syllable *nɛ*, plus object suffixes. Cohen 1936: 148 agrees with this analysis, as does Armbruster 1908: 69 and Leslau 1967: 36. Thus Getatchew's analysis as *n-* + -ɛ appears to be an innovation.

The problem cannot be answered by considering assimilations with the following suffixes because of the Amharic rule ɛ + a → a, e.g. in the 2nd pl., either *n+accihu* or *nɛ+accihu* yields *naccihu*. But consideration of old textual forms may provide a clue. Praetorius 1878 (repr. 1970) lists such forms as *nɛwaccihu*. Could these have arisen from *nɛw + accihu*, *nɛw + accɛw* etc., or was there an Amharic rule of the form ɛ + a → ɛwa at the time?[1]

The other question is the origin of the *n*-copula itself, with or without the -ɛ. Getatchew refers to Praetorius 1878: 258-9 as stating that the origin of *n* may be related to that of the old form *innɛho*, 'Behold!' (Getatchew gives 'be hold!', p. 140, note 2, but this is surely a typographical error). Dawkins 1969: 43, n.1 also suggests that the origin of *nɛw* may be in an interjection 'Behold!' but with no reference. Cohen 1936: 114 refers to "presentative" *innɛho* as being built on the *n* of *nɛw*. Armbruster 1908: 69 gives *nɛ* as having the meaning 'look!, see!' Probably the idea of the "presentative" *nɛ* in modern books traces back to Praetorius in all cases, though not acknowledged.

In fact, the *n* may be ancient in Afroasiatic. I suggest that it may be related to the deictic *n* found in Epigraphic South Arabian and other Semitic languages (Ullendorff 1955: 8-9, n. 30, esp. p. 9) or to the *n~l~r* linking particle in Afroasiatic (Bender 1975: 36). The -ε may be a result of *n*+obj. suffixes being modelled on the most frequent ones *n*+-*ň* (1 sg.), *n*+-*w* (3 m. sg.); and *n*+-*n* (1 pl.) where the expected automatic linking vowel -*i*- is replaced by -ε- because the sequences -*iň* -*iw*, and *in*, are not favored in Amharic in the case of object suffixes (suggested by Grover Hudson, p.c.).

As far as I am concerned, the lengthy attempt to motivate the copula as *n* + ε obj. suf. by structures of the form

   [NP [NP VP]]
   S S   S S

is unnecessary: I am convinced without this discussion, and I find the derivations involving branching diagrams and embeddings down to three or more levels (as in Getatchew's (22), (23), (43), etc.) unconvincing. It is not always clear to me just how to interpret such derivations, and since they seem largely irrelevant, I will make no further comment on them.

However, Getatchew could have thrown more light on the Amharic copula by referring to several really relevant pieces of literature. Noting on the second page of the article (p. 140) that Amharic is the only SOV language of the lot, I immediately thought this might be relevant. In fact, Polotsky pointed out strong parallels between Amharic and Turkish syntax in an earlier Rome conference on Ethiopian studies (Polotsky 1960), and Ferguson 1972 specifically deals with the copula in SOV languages. Getatchew's brief discussion of the use of *honε*, 'be, become', and *allε*, 'be, exist' (149-150) and some other minor matters is largely redundant when one considers the parallel behavior in Bengali and other SOV languages (see esp. Ferguson 1972: 110 for a really striking table of comparison of Bengali and Amharic verbs of being).

Another parallel to the behavior of *nεw*, *allε*, and impersonal verbs generally strikes me as illuminating. In Russian, possession is shown by the construction prep. + pronoun (in prepositional case) + zero copula + possessed, e.g. *u meňa kniga*, 'I have a book' (lit. 'to me a book'). With this wealth of parallels, we do not need elaborate transformational machinery to justify analyzing Amharic copulas as impersonal verb constructions!

The article is well-written and the lapses in English are few. It might be helpful to the reader to point out a few typos and lapses I noted, in addition to two already mentioned earlier. On p. 140, just before the list of pronominal suffixes, I do not know what ". . . copula are given in (1)" refers to unless (1) should have been (9). On p. 141, ex. (14), "Almaz", not "Almas"; ex. (15) "A thief stole my money," not ". . . me money." P. 142, line 2, "prepositional phrase," not propositional phrase." P. 143, text above ex. (25), does it mean "which happens in the case of a sentence with an intransitive verb and no prepositional phrase".? P. 144, ex. (28), in the diagram, NP, not PN. P. 145, ex. (30) *wättadäru*, not *wättädäru*. P. 147, ex. (41a), *mämhir*, not *nämhir*. P. 149, ex. (47)b, *mämhir*, not *mämbir*. P. 152, just above ex. (62a), reference should be to Abraham and Hailu 1970, not Abraham Hailu.

In reading papers written in the Semitist tradition, I am always frustrated by the habit of listing paradigms in the order beginning with 3 m. sg: maybe it is an ethnocentric objection, but I note that most modern grammars of Amharic have shifted to the "logical" sequence beginning with 1 sg. The basic 3 m. sg. can be seen just as easily in this sequence, and paradigms are brought into line with non-Semitist usage. I am even more frustrated by the adoption of a transcription using the clumsy *ä* for the most frequent vowel in Amharic (the first-order vowel which I represent by ε) and the misleading *ə* for the high-central vowel (which I represent by *i*). If *ə* must be used, it would make more sense to use *ə* for the first-order vowel and ordinary *i* for the high-central (with *ī* then being used for the high-front).[2]

Aside from minor quibbles and trying to suggest some further steps one might take in the directions indicated by this thoughtful article, my main criticism is aimed at "overkill." It is not often that one's main objection is that the author presented too much evidence to convince one of his argument. I hope my comments are interpreted as constructive ones, since I want to conclude on a positive note: I enjoyed reading Getatchew's article and I was gratified at having an opportunity to study in some depth this example of the insightful work now being done by Ethiopian professional linguists on the analysis of Amharic.

FOOTNOTES:

[1] Grover Hudson (private communication) suggests also the possibility of *ni+accɛw → nɛwaccɛw*. I want to thank Grover for reading and criticizing the first draft of this review. He is not responsible for any errors of fact or interpretation contained therein.

[2] (ADDED BY THE EDITOR): This problem of transcription has already been the object of a private debate between Dr. Bender and myself, and since he has now chosen to publish his ideas on it, I feel it necessary to add my own comments. Calling ä "clumsy" is a statement of esthetic content, and, thus, highly subjective. ɛ is a Greek letter, definitely clumsier in a Latin script. Furthermore, it is phonetically incorrect. [ɛ] is the transcription used for the vowel of French *faire* which is by no means identical with the half-open central "first" vowel of Amharic. The closest IPA symbol would be ɐ (in fact it is used by some British scholars), but ä is in no contradiction with IPA: ".." as a modifier is used with central vowels in general. The symbol *i* evokes unnecessary associations with *i*, whereas ə is a generally used symbol for the *schwa*, the essentially euphonic vowel that alternates with zero. Both ä and ə are time-honored symbols, used by many specialists in the field, and there is no reason for suddenly rejecting them. Robert Hetzron

REFERENCES: (in addition to those listed by the author)

Armbruster, C.H., 1908 - *Initia Amharica*, Vol. 1, Cambridge University Press.

Bender, M.L., 1975 - *Omotic: A New Afroasiatic Language Family*, Southern Illinois University Museum Series No. 3, Carbondale.

Cohen, Marchel, 1936 - *Traité de langue amharique*, (reprinted by Altai Reprints, 1970).

Dawkins, C.H. 1960 (repr. 1969) - *The Fundamentals of Amharic*, Sudan Interior Mission, Addis Ababa.

Ferguson, C.A., 1972 - "Verbs of 'Being' in Bengali, with a Note on Amharic," vol. 5 in John W. H. Verhaar (ed)., *The Verb 'be' and its Synonyms*, (Foundations of Language Supplementary Series 14) Reidel, Dordrecht.

Getatchew Haile, 1972 - "The Copula   (näw) in Amharic," *IV Congresso Internazionale di Studi Etiopic*, Accademia Nazionale dei Lincei, Rome.

Leslau, Wolf, 1967 - *Amharic Textbook*, Otto Harrassowitz, Wiesbaden.

Polotsky, H.J., 1960 - "Syntaxe Amharique et Syntaxe Turque," *Atti del Convegno Internazionale di Studi Etiopici*, Accademia Nazionale dei Lincei, Rome.

Praetorius, Franz, 1878 - *Die Amharische Sprache*, Verlag der Buchhandlung des Waisenhauses, Halle. (Reprint 1970 by Georg Olms Verlag, Hilderschein, N.Y.)

Ullendorff, Edward, 1955 - *The Semitic Languages of Ethiopia*, Taylor's Foreign Press, London.

3.3. HABTE MARIAM MARCOS, "Palatalization in Ennemor," in *IV Congresso Internazionale di Studi Etiopici (Roma, 10-15 aprile 1972)*, Tomo II, (Sezione Linguistica; Problemi Attuali di Scienze e di Cultura, 191). Rome: Accademia Nazionale dei Lincei, 1974.

By C. DOUGLAS JOHNSON (University of California, Santa Barbara)

Habte attempts a generative account of palatalization and certain related phenomena in Ennemor, an Ethiopian Semitic language of the Western Gurage group. The accepted practice in such descriptions is to formulate each rule explicitly and unambiguously, even if informally, and to discuss the evidence for the rule and the motivation for its significant details. Occasionally derivations are given for illustrative or probative purposes. In any case the explicit formulation of the rule is done separately from the display of any particular derivation; the rules applied in a derivation are referred to not by the formulations themselves, which may be rather cumbersome, but rather by convenient and uniform names or numbers used consistently throughout.

H. has chosen a rather different and more confusing format. Except for a brief and incomplete summary at the end of his paper, H. introduces explicit rules only as comments accompanying lines in a derivation. These comments may be anything from names of general processes to detailed formulations. The process names are uninformative because they are not defined specifically for Ennemor (e.g. Metathesis on p. 261, Vowel Harmony on p. 260, Epenthesis on p. 256 and 260), while the detailed formulations result in great redundancy of exposition because, not being attached to names, they must be repeated every time a rule applies (though H. does sometimes avoid this by saying that step *n* of one derivation is like step *m* of another). This redundancy might be harmless if inelegant and might even help the reader were it not that H. formulates the same rule differently on different occasions. A good example is a rule I will call Raising, which appears in all of the following guises: "a low vowel before high continuant suffixes is raised" (p. 253); "a low vowel before a palatal continuant is raised" (p. 26o); "a low vowel before a high continuant is raised" (p. 261); "a low vowel before a high back continuant is raised" (p. 263); "the stressed vowel before the palatal continuant is raised" (p. 264). The third version of the rule seems to be the best candidate for a definitive statement, since in the actual derivations the vowel being raised is always *a* and the continuant is always *y* or *w*. But H. does not help us toward this conclusion. It is left to the reader to examine the derivations and reconcile the discrepant rule formulations.

Poor presentation of this sort plays havoc with one of H's main theses. He assumes "in all cases that stress, or absence of it, is significant for the proper derivation of phonetic forms" (p. 264). One would therefore expect a full and coherent treatment of stress in preparation for the main topic. Instead one finds only scattered and inconsistent references to it in derivations. Apart from stress marks in cited forms, the first mention of stress is as a conditioning factor in a vowel-fronting rule on pp. 253-4. Not until p. 256 do we find out that there are stress rules, and even then we do not get a clear picture of what they are. We find, for example, the following: "The penultimate syllable before an open syllable is stressed" (p. 256); "Stress is assigned to the last closed syllable" (p. 259); "The penultimate syllable is stressed" (p. 260); "Word-final closed syllable is stressed" (p. 260). Rule ordering is no more consistent. One finds penultimate stress already marked in underlying representations (*ä+gɜ́ṛy* in the middle of p. 256), assigned by rule prior to Raising (derivation /e/ near top of p. 260), assigned by an unknown mechanism simultaneously with Raising (middle of p. 253), and assigned by rule after Raising (derivation /a/ on p. 261). If H. had a good reason for changing his mind so often, he doesn't tell us what it is.

There is even an unexplained instance of apparent cyclic application (p. 259), though it is not called that. The Sg. 3m. perfect *sêʔä* 'look for' is derived simply enough from *säʔyä+ä*, there being one application of a stress rule. The Pl. 3m. of the same verb is then derived as follows. First, *sêʔä* is derived from *säʔyä* in the manner previously described,

except that there is no final +*ä* to be deleted. Then the composite form *sê?ä+w+m* is turned
into *s?ŏm*ʷ by a series of rules of which one assigns final stress. The controversial nature
of word-internal cycles in phnology would lead one to expect some supporting argumentation
for this derivation, but none is forthcoming from H.

For a clear and complete formulation of the stress rules the reader must turn to Hetzron 1970,
not cited by H. The basic rule is very simple and noncyclic: a word ending in a nonfront
vowel has stress on the next to last vowel (if there is one); any other word has stress on the
last vowel. For this purpose long vowels must be regarded as geminate vowels. A more complex
situation arises when certain suffixes are present. The so-called M-morpheme, for example, is
manifested by stress on the last two vowels when added to words of a certain well-defined
class. To this class belong Sg. 3m. perfects of the form CäCäCä; e.g. compare the subordinate
verb *säpärä* 'break', which lacks the M-morpheme, with the main verb *säpärä̃*, which contains
the M-morpheme. This phenomenon may account in part for the variety of stress patterns H.
assigns without explanation to Sg. 3m. perfects, e.g. *dämädä̃* 'unite', *näkådä̃* 'touch' (p. 257),
nämädä̃ 'like' (p. 257).

The substance of H.'s paper is difficult to discern because of its organizational defects,
merely sampled above. Fortunately, though, he does summarize what he considers the four most
important rules at the end (p. 265). Quoted verbatim, these rules are:

1. Dentals that precede a stressless palatal continuant or a back continuant are
   palatalized.

2. Velars that precede a stressless palatal continuant suffix are palatalized, provided that a stop does not intervene between them.

3. Where there are no palatalizable consonants, the stressed vowel before the palatal
   continuant is fronted.

4. The palatalizing segment is elided.

Good examples from pp. 253-3 are the singular imperatives

masculine	feminine	
wŏsd	*wŏsĵ*	'take'
kəɓŏɓ	*kʸəɓŏɓ*	'trim'
sərŏm	*sərim*	'spin'

H. assumes that the underlying representation of the feminine imperatives consists of the
masculine imperative plus a suffix -*y*. Neglecting stress for the moment, I infer that he
derives feminines in part as follows:

wəsd+y	*kəɓəɓ+y*	*sərəm+y*	
wəsĵ+y	- - -	- - -	1
- - -	*kʸəɓəɓ+y*	- - -	2
- - -	- - -	*sərim+y*	3
wəsĵ	*kʸəɓəɓ*	*sərim*	4

I have no great quarrel with the general content of rules 1 - 4 or their ordering, but must
object to the looseness of their formulation. In general rule 1 can palatalize only a dental
that IMMEDIATELY precedes a palatal continuant; e.g. *t* is not palatalized in *kətiɓ* (*kətəɓ+y*)
'hash (sg. f. imperative)'. The one exception is that the vowel *ä* (or perhaps any vowel)
may intervene. For example, the sg. f. imperative *ɓŏĵä* 'unfasten' must be derived from
ɓəda+y in H.'s framework (p. 253). The change of *a* to *ä* can be attributed to Raising. Rule 1

must then apply to yield ɣəǰä̆+y, but can do so only if its structural description contains an optional vowel (perhaps just ä) before the conditioning palatal continuant. That is, if we ignore for this discussion the possible palatalizing effect of a back continuant, we must formalize rule 1 approximately as follows:

(a)   [+cor]   →   [+pal]   /   ——   (V) $\begin{bmatrix} +pal \\ +cont \end{bmatrix}$

The output ɣəǰä̆+y must now become ɣə́ǰä, but this outcome is possible only if rule 4 precedes the basic stress rule. Otherwise we would have ɣəǰä̆+y by the stress rule and then ɣəǰä́ by rule 4. H. apparently overlooks this fact, or has some other formulation of the stress rule(s) in mind, since he usually introduces stress before the elision of y in derivations; cf. the derivations /a/ and /c/ on the second half of p. 259, derivation /e/ near the top of page 260, and the derivation of the gerundive ɣəǰä̆ätä from ɣədaa+ytä on p. 264.

In contrast to rule 1, rule 2 palatalizes a velar which is at ANY distance from a palatal continuant occurring later in the same word; cf. kʸəɣɔ́ɣ above. In H.'s data an intervening t, r, š, or ž blocks the palatalization but an intervening vowel, β, ɣ, n, or ʔ demonstrably does not; cf. the following sg. f. imperatives:

UNDERLYING	PHONETIC	
kətəɣ+y	kətĭɣ	'hash'
ḳərəm+y	ḳərĭm	'insult'
nəks+y	nə́kš̆	'bite'
gaʔaz+y	gaʔä́ž̆	'move'
gəbʔa+y	gʸə́βʔä	'enter'
ḳänɣa+y	ḳʸä̆nɣä	'knock'

The reason for thinking that š and ž block velar palatalization is that nə́kš and gaʔä́ž are derived from intermediate nəkš+y, gaʔäž+y, produced by rule 1; the glottal stop in gaʔäž+y cannot be regarded as the blocking element because it does not block palatalization in gʸə́βʔä. I should note in passing that I have departed slightly from H.'s transcription of the latter form; he writes all β as b on the assumption of a rule eventually turning noninitial b into β (p. 252; there are exceptions however, e.g. ṭäbäṭä 'he seized'). I have been unable to find crucial evidence concerning the possible blocking effect of other consonants in the sources available to me. Clearly, though, H. is imprecise when he implies that all and only stops (or nonnasal continuants (p. 252)) do the blocking. One possibility consistent with the data is that the blocking consonants are the nonnasal coronals. Accordingly, rule 2 might be formulated approximately as follows:

(b) $\begin{bmatrix} +cons \\ -ant \\ -cor \end{bmatrix}$ →   [+pal]   /   —— $\begin{bmatrix} \left\{ \begin{matrix} +nas \\ -cor \end{matrix} \right\} \end{bmatrix}_0$ + $\begin{bmatrix} +cont \\ +pal \\ +suf \end{bmatrix}$

Previously cited examples (səɾĭm, kətĭɣ, ḳərĭm) show that rule 3 will front a vowel separated from a following palatal continuant by a consonant. In fact in all examples I can find there is at least one intervening consonant. The sg. f. imperatives ʔĭβä 'run' and sĭmʔä, 'hear', which are derived in H.'s system from ʔəba+y and səmʔa+y, show that rule 3 too must have an optional vowel before the palatal continuant in its structural description. H. says that the presence of a palatalizable consonant blocks rule 3, but this statement seems equivocal; š is palatalizable in the sense that it can be palatalized by rule 1 in the appropriate context, but in səɾĭm, where it is not actually palatalized, it does not prevent rule 3 from applying. What he meant perhaps was that a palatalized consonant (or more specifically a consonant palatalized by rule 1 or 2) will, if present, block rule 3. Building this restriction into the rule we arrive at the following approximate formulation:

(c) V → [-back] / #[-pal]$_0$ ——— $\begin{bmatrix} C \\ -pal \end{bmatrix}_1$ (V) $\begin{bmatrix} +cont \\ +pal \\ +suf \end{bmatrix}$

The rules as we have stated them will correctly derive the imperatives *ʔíβä* and *sím ʔä*. Not only that but the gerundive, formed from the 2nd sg. imperative by the addition of *tä*, will also be correctly derived. Derivations of 'hear' demonstrate this.

SG. F. IMPERATIVE	GERUNDIVE	
səm ʔa+y	*səm ʔa+ytä*	
səm ʔä+y	*səm ʔä+ytä*	Raising
sím ʔä+y	*sím ʔä+ytä*	3 (formulated as (c))
sím ʔä	*sím ʔätä*	4

The basic stress rule will yield the actual forms *sím ʔä* and *sím ʔätä* (the latter kindly supplied by Robert Hetzron) if now applied to the output of 4. Stress assignment clearly must follow rule 4, for otherwise it would produce the imperative *sim ʔä+y*, ultimately *sím ʔä*. This ordering is of course the same as that needed to derive *ʃə́jä*, discussed in connection with rule 1 above, and seems therefore to be well supported.

H.'s assumption that rule 3 follows stress assignment and fronts only stressed vowels is, on the other hand, untenable. He would have to reformulate the stress rule so as to ignore a word-final *y* and even then he could not derive the gerundives *ʔíβätä* and *sím ʔätä* correctly because those words contain unstressed vowels that are nevertheless fronted by rule 3.

H. implies that all palatal continuants induce Raising, palatalization, and fronting, but in fact the only palatal continuant that does so is *y*. Other high front continuants, which would also be called palatal in some terminologies, do not have these effects. For example, the suffixes -*i* and -*ša*, both of which begin with a stressless high front (and therefore palatal?) continuant at the time rule 1 is supposed to apply, fail to palatalize the *d* in *biidí* 'at home' (p. 264) and *biidša* 'her home' (Hetzron 1970:574). H. to be sure, says that only a stressless palatal continuant can trigger rule 1, but in fact the -*i* in *biidí* must be stressless when that rule applies because stress assignment has to take place after rule 4, as we showed above. In any case H.'s proposed ordering would not explain the absence of palatalization in *biidša*. H. ought to have defined the palatalizing segment as a palatal glide or palatal semivowel.

H. neglects on the whole to consider alternative hypotheses. The prominent exception concerns the behavior of *r* in a palatalizing environment (pp. 253-4), illustrated by the sg. f. imperatives *xʷê* 'go', *xǽ* 'know', *səβí* 'break', derived from underlying *xʷär+y*, *xar+y*, *səbər+y*, respectively. One proposal is that *r* is palatalized by rule 1 like any other coronal, its only peculiarity being that its palatalized counterpart is *y*. An independently motivated late rule of Contraction, which converts a vowel + *y* sequence into a front vowel (p. 264), yields the phonetic forms. For example:

səbər+y	
səbəy+y	rule 1
səbəy	rule 4
səbi	Contraction
səβi	noninitial *b* → β

Another proposal exempts *r* from palatalization and postulates a late rule deleting *r* after a front vowel; e.g.

səbər+y	
səbir+y	rule 3
səbir	rule 4

ѕəbᴉ   ʀ-deletion
ѕəβᴉ   noninitial *b → β*

H. favors the second proposal and argues against the first as follows. (1) Certain forms
contain an unpalatalized *ʀ* in what H. claims is a palatalizing environment, e.g. *xaʀᴉ*
'intelligent', *j̆ɔ̈ʀä* 'a limper', *bʷänäʀmʷ* 'fly (pl. 3m. perfect)', and (2) a vowel is fronted
before palatalized *ʀ* but not before other palatalized coronals. It is hard to accept these
arguments, however. The first one undermines both proposals equally. If *ʀ* is really in a
palatalizing environment in the examples cited, both proposals, unless further restricted,
would predict the incorrect forms *xeᴉ, *j̆ᴉä, *bʷäném̃*. H. would have to argue that the necessary
further restriction is more easily and naturally incorporated into the second proposal than
the first, but he does not do so. The second argument would be valid only if the first proposal predicted vowel fronting before all palatalized coronals. But it makes no such prediction. It predicts apparent fronting before palatalized *ʀ* only because palatalized *ʀ*, being a
y, triggers Contraction. It does not predict fronting before any other palatalized coronal,
because neigher rule 3 nor Contraction can apply there. Where the first proposal actually
fails is in predicting the following incorrect derivation:

xaʀ+y	
xay+y	rule 1
xʸay+y	rule 2
xʸay	rule 4
xʸæ	Contraction

Still, any number of plausible adjustments could correct this defect in the first proposal.
Perhaps velars are later depalatalized before a front vowel. Alternatively, rule 1 might
merely make coronals [+high, -back], leaving the additional changes in place and manner of
articulation to a later rule; this is a question both H. and I have skirted by subsuming the
whole process under the traditional term "palatalization." Rule 1 would then produce *ʀʸ, tʸ,*
dʸ, etc., instead of *y, č, j̆* directly. More particularly, it would convert *xaʀ+y* to *xaʀʸ+y*,
which would not be subject to rule 2 as formulated in (b).

Repeated radicals in verbs of the root form 122 or 1212 will both be palatalized if the second
one is palatalized by rules so far discussed. Consequently we have sg. f. imperatives such
as *ѕəžɔ̆ž* 'feel better', *mäžmɔ̈ž* 'worry'. H.'s description of this fact (p. 252) is clear enough
but is marred by a number of misprints in the data; thus his rule requires that we read *äkʸɔ̆kʸ,*
bäʀgʸɔ̆gʸ, nəj̆äj̆, kʸäѕkʸɔ̆ѕ for printed *äkʸɔ̆k, bäʀgʸɔ̆g, nədäj̆, käѕkʸɔ̆ѕ*. H. wisely refrains from
trying to formalize the mechanism responsible for this double palatalization. The type
/ѕəzɔ̆z+y/ → *ѕəžɔ̆ž* probably results from a rule which says that a consonant becomes identical
to the next following consonant if it can do so merely by acquiring a secondary articulation
(along with the automatic concommittants such as affrication and loss of anteriority); cf. the
similar phenomenon in Chaha which I discuss elsewhere (Johnson, 1975). The type /mäzmɔ̂ž/ →
mäžmɔ̂ž, considered as containing a reduplicated root *mz*, could be explained along the lines
by Wilbur (1973), in connection with a number of other languages. Either the reduplication
takes place after the palatalization rules or else derivations "remember" what consonants are
duplicates of each other so that the palatalization rules can affect both of them. Wilbur
makes a strong cross-linguistic case for the latter type of mechanism, explaining the phenomenon
as part of a tendency to preserve the phonological similarity of the reduplicated parts.

H. discusses a few other palatalizing elements in addition to the sg. fem. imperative and
gerundive. We will confine our remarks to root-final *y*, which he deals with only in the special
case where the next preceding consonant is *ʀ*. An illustrative example is the verb 'cast a
spell' (pp. 255-256):

UNDERLYING	PHONETIC	
gäʀyä	*gä̆ň̆ä̆*	sg. 3m. perfect
y+gäʀy	*yəgê*	sg. 3m. imperfect

y+gäṛy	yəgʷäṛúa	pl. 3m. imperfect
ä+gəṛy	ägî	sg. 3m. jussive
ä+gəṛy+wa	ägʷəṛúa	pl. 3m. jussive

The derivation of gä̃n̆ä̃ involves an uncontroversial change of ṛ to n in the perfect according to a morphological rule, followed by palatalization of the n. The double accent is due to the M-morpheme; without that morpheme the verb would be gä̃n̆ä. An Epenthesis rule, never formulated or explained by H., is supposed to break up the initial yg cluster in the imperfect. This rule and other rules previously discussed are all that are needed to derive the non-perfect singular forms. To give the flavor of H.'s work I quote in full his derivations of the plural forms (p. 256):

/i/	y+gaṛy+wa	
/j/	yəgäṛywa	(Epenthesis).
/k/	yəgäṛwa	(A palatal continuant before a back continuant is elided).
/l/	yəgaṛəwa	(Epenthesis).
/m/	yəgäṛə́wa	(The penultimate syllable before an open syllable is stressed).
/n/	yəgʷäṛə́wa	(A velar before a labial continuant is rounded).
/o/	yəgʷäṛúwa	(A stressed central vowel before a back rounded continuant is rounded).
	ä+gəṛy+wa	
	ägəṛwa	(Same as /k/).
	ägəṛəwa	(Same as /l/).
	ägʷəṛə́wa	(Same as /m/).
	ägʷəṛə́wa	(Same as /n/).
	ägʷəṛúa	(Same as /o/).

There are two derivations here, one beginning at line /i/ and the other beginning at the line next after /o/. The first a in lines /i/ and /l/ is a misprint for ä. The first derivation does not end with the desired output yəgʷäṛúa. The second derivation does end with the desired output, but H. does not explain how the w is lost. Step /n/ involves the well-known process of Internal Labialization, described in Hetzron and Habte 1966; and in Hetzron 1971. The rule at step /k/ may be perfectly valid (it occurs in a number of derivations), but H. makes no overt attempt to support its existence. Since H. nowhere explains, motivates, or formulates Epenthesis, we are left wondering why Epenthesis in the first derivation applies both before and after another rule but fails to break up the ṛyw cluster on the first application.

The verb fä̃n̆ä̃ 'fear' also contains a root of the form Cṛy, according to H., but has sg. 3m. jussive äfṛê instead of the afî one might expect an analogy with gä̃n̆ä/ägî. H. indicates in the relevant tables (pp. 255-6) that he would derive äfṛê from ä+fṛäy but does not explain how he would reconcile this proposal with his treatment of the sg. f. imperative, which assumes that final -äy existing prior to application of rule 1 is realized phonetically as unstressed -ä.

The 3m. perfects sîyää (sg.), səṛä̃ä̃umʷ (pl.) 'buy' (pp. 260-1) represent a somewhat different type. H. would derive the singular as follows (p. 261; an umlaut missing in H. is restored in the next-to-last step):

/a/ *sᵊraayä*

    sᵊrääyä   (A low vowel before a high continuant is raised).

    sᵊryäää   (Metathesis).

    sᵊryä   (A long vowel in a word final position is always shortened).

    sə́ryä   (Stress is assigned to the penultimate syllable).

    síryä   (A stressed vowel before a palatal continuant is fronted).

    síyä   (An alveolar flap after a fronted vowel drops).

The first, fourth, and fifth rules represent respectively Raising, the basic stress rule, and rule 3, whose formulation and ordering I have already commented on. H. says nothing further on Metathesis, which he invokes only for this and a couple of similar verbs. The rule that applies next is puzzling since the desired output form was supposed to have been *síyää*, so cited by H. on p. 260. The last rule, *r*-deletion, is valid to the extent that H.'s analysis of *ry* clusters is valid. What is missing is an explanation of why rule 4 does not delete the *y*, which is the palatalizing segment that induces the fronting of the schwa. Perhaps rule 4 must be restricted so as not to apply to intervocalic *y*'s. If one supposes, contrary to H., that the *r* before the *y* is palatalized by rule 1 one faces a similar problem, since Contraction should give *siä* from *sᵊyä*, derived in turn from *sᵊryä* by rules 1 and 4. Perhaps Contraction should be broken up into two rules, one of which fronts a vowel immediately before -*y* and the other of which deletes syllable final -*y* after a front vowel.

H. does not formulate, explain, or explicitly motivate the rule of Metathesis. If he can actually demonstrate the existence of this rule in, say, the generalized form

$$\text{C} \quad \overset{\vee}{\text{V}}_0 \quad y \quad \rightarrow \quad 1 \quad 3 \quad 2$$
$$1 \quad 2 \quad 3$$

he has missed the opportunity to make an interesting point. For if Metathesis applies between Raising and rule 1 then neither rule 1 nor rule 3 need allow for an optional vowel before the palatalizing segment; in other words the "(V)" can be dropped from our formalizations in (a) and (c). Such forms as *fə̌ǰä* and *sim?ä̀tä* would then be derived as follows:

fᵊda+y	*səm?a+ytä*	
fᵊdä+y	*səm?ä+ytä*	Raising
fᵊdyä	*səm?yätä*	Metathesis
fᵊǰyä	———	Rule 1 ((a) without "(V)")
———	*sim?yä̀tä*	Rule 3 ((c) without "(V)")
fə̌ǰä	*sim?ä̀tä*	Rule 4

So far I have assumed that rule 4 follows rules 1-3 in a strict linear ordering. An interesting alternative is that rule 4 is actually unordered, applying anytime the appropriate conditions arise. Possibly, even, rule 4 is a language-specific metarule that says that each of the rules 1-3 automatically deletes a segment matching the palatalizing *y* in its structural description. The problem would thereby be solved of how to distinguish palatalizing segments, which rule 4 elides, from other *y*'s (e.g. the initial *y*'s of imperfect forms), which remain. At any rate, whether 4 is an unordered rule or a metarule, the consequences would be these. First, rule 2 could be formulated more in accord with H.'s apparent intentions, since the blocking segments could be defined as the consonantal nonnasal noncontinuants in the sense of Jakobson, Fant, and Halle (1952), for whom a tap or a trill such as Ennemor *r* is noncontinuant. Rules 1 and 4 together would then turn underlying /nᵊks+y/ and /ga?az+y/ immediately into *nᵊkš* and *ga?až*, respectively, thereby bleeding rule 2 regardless of how the blocking consonants are defined. Secondly, the first proposal for dealing with *r*'s in palatalizing environments could be maintained, since derivation of x*ǽ* could proceed as follows if *r* is palatalized to *y* by rule 1:

xar+y

xay   rules 1 & 4

———   rule 2 (inapplicable because there is no longer a suffixal *y*)

x *æ*   Contraction

Thirdly, rule 3 could be simplified because it would no longer have to be sensitive to the presence or absence of palatalized consonants in the input word. These and previous considerations lead to the following formulations of rules 1-3:

(d) $[+\text{cor}]$ → $[+\text{pal}]$ / ——— y (rule 1)

(e) $\begin{bmatrix} -\text{cor} \\ +\text{cons} \\ -\text{ant} \end{bmatrix}$ → $[+\text{pal}]$ / ——— $\begin{bmatrix} \left\{ \begin{matrix} +\text{nas} \\ +\text{cont} \\ -\text{cons} \end{matrix} \right\} \end{bmatrix}$ $+ y$ (rule 2)

(f) V → $[-\text{back}]$ / ——— $C_0 y$ (rule 3)

Rules 1 and 3 now look like completely natural palatalization and umlaut rules, respectively. However, no obvious consideration of that sort would support (e) over (b) as a formulation of rule 2. A verb of the root form Velar – Coronal Fricative – Labial would shed more light on the matter. If its sg. f. imperative had a palatalized first radical, then the coronal fricative could not be among the consonants which block rule 2. Formulation (e) would then be supported along with the assumption of an unordered rule 4. On the other hand, if the sg. f. imperative of the hypothetical verb did not have a palatalized first radical, the blocking consonants for rule 2 would have to include at least one coronal fricative, contrary to (e). It would still be possible, of course, to retain an unordered rule 4 and formulations (d)-(f) provided merely that we substitute $[\{+\text{nas}, -\text{cor}\}]$ for the bracketed expression in (e), but the only evidence for this solution would be the supposedly greater naturalness of (d) and (f) over (a) and (c), respectively.

I have not found a verb of the desired form in the sources available to me, and therefore cannot further evaluate the proposals of the preceding paragraphs. With his superior command of the data H. could probably supply such a verb if it exists. Unfortunately he has not done so in his paper because he has failed to realize its significance, having formulated his rules too loosely even to discern the relevant questions.

H. remarks (p. 255), truly but ungrammatically, that "very few languages reflect as a intricate but interesting phonological structure as the dialect of Ennemor does." More is the pity that H. could not shed more light on the really interesting problems or at least describe the facts in a clearer way. I hope someday he will.

REFERENCES

Hetzron, Robert (1970). "Vocalic length and stress in Ennemor," *Le Muséon* 83.559-581.

—————————— (1971). "Internal Labialization in the *tt*-group of Outer South Ethiopic," *Journal of the American Oriental Society* 91.192-207.

Hetzron, Robert and Habte Mariam Marcos (1966). "Des traits pertinents superposés en ennemor," *Journal of Ethiopian Studies* 4.17-30.

Jakobson, R., G. Fant, and M. Halle (1952). *Preliminaries to Speech Analysis*. Cambridge, Mass., MIT Press.

Johnson, C.D. (1975). "Phonological channels in Chaha," *Afroasiatic Linguistics*, 2/2.

Wilbur, Ronnie B. (1973). "The phonology of reduplication," reproduced by the Indiana University Linguistics Club.

3.4. GOLDENBREG, GIDEON, "L'étude du gourague et la comparaison chamito-semitique," in *IV Congresso Internazionale di Studi Etiopici (Roma, 10-15 aprile 1972)*, Tomo II, (Sezione Linguistica; Problemi Attuali di Scienza e di Cultura, 191). Rome: Accademia Nazionale dei Lincei, 1974, pp. 235-249.
By ROBERT HETZRON (University of California, Santa Barbara)

The main scope of the article is to present arguments against the hypothesis that the Main Verb-Marker endings of Soddo, Goggot and Muher (-u, -i, -t, -n/-tt) are of proto-Semitic origin and related to the Arabic indicative endings -u and -n(V). The possibility of such a relationship between the two was first mentioned by W. Leslau (the last time in *JNES* 26.121-5, 1967), and further developed by the present reviewer (*Africa* 38.156-72, (1968); *BSOAS* 35.451-75, (1972)). One finds a striking distributional resemblance between them, Arabic *yaksir-u* 'he breaks' *yaksiru:-na* 'they break' (-u after consonant, -nV after a long vowel) vs. Soddo-Goggot-Muher *yəsäbr-u* 'he breaks', Soddo-Goggot *yəsäbrəmu-n*, but Muher *yəsäbrəmu-tt* 'they break'. The latter -tt constitutes a difference in the set of allomorphs used; furthermore, as against Arabic *taksir-u* 'she breaks', Soddo, Goggot and Muher have *təsäbr-i* (with an -i), and these languages have after third person complement suffixes an ending -t (*yəsäbər-rə-t* 'he breaks it') unparallelled by Arabic (which does not allow the insertion of any element between the indicative endings and the verbal stem).

In the following, I shall take up Goldenberg's main arguments against the proto-Semitic hypothesis (i.e. the suggestion that the Soddo-Goggot-Muher endings and the Arabic ones are related) point by point, with my reply to them.

(I) In Northern Gurage (a convenient term to be used for the three Ethiopian languages involved), the Main Verb-Markers are SEPARABLE from the verbal stem by complement suffixes, which is not the case in Arabic, cf. Northern Gurage *yəsäbər-š-u* 'he+breaks-you(f.sg.)-MVM' vs. Arabic *yaksir-u-ki* 'he+breaks-Ind.-you(f.sg.)'. Goldenberg first suggests that the separability of the Sg.3m. possessive ending of Soddo (e.g. *məšt-əmm-u* 'wife-and-his' for 'and his wife') makes its relation with the corresponding proto-Semitic ending *-hu(:) problematic. Note that all the other possessive endings in these languages are, clearly, reduced independent pronouns and not continuations of the Semitic possessive endings, and the insertability between them and the stem may be a remnant of the period when they were more independent phonologically, i.e. when the construction was still 'house of-I', etc. The Sg.3m. possessive endings may, after all, also be of independent pronominal element. Now, coming back to the Main Verb-Markers, it was not my contention that the Northern Gurage endings actually come from an Arabic-type well-cliticized suffix, but that they are of a copular-auxiliary origin, and while Arabic had strongly fused them with the verbal stem, Northern Gurage has maintained a trace of the older stage when they were independent words. One finds a similar case in written Portuguese. The Romance future endings are cliticized forms for the verb 'have': *scribere habeo* → Spanish *escribiré* 'I shall write', an inseparable word. Yet, while Spanish has *le escribiré* 'I shall write to him', with 'to him' as an outside element added, written Portuguese still has *escrever-lhe-ei* 'write-to+him-I+will'. The analogy with Northern Gurage is perfect.

(II) Arabic has the indicative endings also in negation. In Northern Gurage negative verbal forms reflect a more ARCHAIC shape of the verb (e.g. *säbbärä* 'he broke', but *al-säbärä* 'he did not break', with no gemination of the mid radical), and they do not carry Main Verb-Markers. Now, first of all, the archaic character of these negative forms go back to proto-South-Ethiopic, whereas we are dealing with an incomparably longer time-depth: proto-Semitic. In the case of such remote relationships it is no wonder that there are functional and distributional differences. Rundgren has already observed (*Intensiv und Aspektkorrelation*, p. 242) that the Main Verb-Markers are used in much the same fashion as the auxiliary *-all* in Amharic. These endings follow the Cushitic pattern of verbal morphology which clearly distinguishes main and subordinate forms, and has negative forms radically different from the corresponding affirmative ones. Thus, the proto-Semitic endings were reorganized in a Cushitic manner, — which is by no means surprising in Ethiopian. I agree with Goldenberg that the oldest attested Ethiopian Semitic language: Ge'ez, shows no traces of such endings, but I have already suggested elsewhere that the split of proto-Ethiopian into a Northern group (including Ge'ez, Tigrinya and Tigre) must have greatly antedated the first attestation of Ge'ez, thus there was plenty of time for it to give up the original ending so that it would be unrecoverable through internal reconstruction.

(III) This is where Goldenberg describes the Main Verb-Markers in Soddo and Muher. He points out that in Soddo only the past auxiliary *näbbär(ä)* 'was' appears without such Markers, which parallels the lack of *-m* after the corresponding verb in Chaha: *banä* (while all the other past tense verbs in a main position have *-m*). He also mentions the curious prohibitive form that consists of *ən-* followed by past tense forms provided with Main Verb-Markers. These facts are surely interesting and deserve investigation, but they all belong to a late level in the development of the language. It is to be suspected that a good morphological study of the substratum languages may provide some kind of an explanation. Yet, clearly, these are of little relevance for the "proto-Semitic hypothesis."

(IV) Goldenberg quotes Rundgren and mentions that proto-Semitic final short *-u* (as in Arabic *yaksir-u*) is supposed to have become ϕ in Ethiopian, hence the improbability of this origin for an actual final *-u* in Northern Gurage. Yet, (a) elements with a function that is meant to be preserved may often resist regular phonetic changes, (b) the relatively independent status: separability from the verbstem (see (I) above), may have also contributed to its survival: it had more prosodic independence and was not truly suffixal at the time final short vowels were reduced. The fact that the distributional features of *-u* and *-n* (the latter after original long vowels) are not limited to these endings but are also found in complement suffix pronouns is not surprising, —a stem-final consonant vs. a stem-final long vowel provide so different environments for subsequent suffixes, that a divergent allomorphic development based on these two environments in several instances is to be expected. (IV.4): There is no doubt that the Soddo forms of the endings are the result of a long and complicated development and synchronically differ from the Arabic endings. Yet all the deviations can be explained: Sg.3f. *-i* inspired by the labial/palatal opposition of genders in independent pronouns (Arabic *huwa/hiya*), Sg.2f. *-in* coming from a metanalysis after an original suffix *-i:. The fact that the personal ending *-mu* of Pl.2/em. has been reduced to *-m* in Soddo (in final position), whereas *-mu* is still possible as a sequence of a final radical *-u* and a Main Verb-Marker - is quite normal in the light of what one knows about the conditioning power of morphemic boundaries in many languages.

(V) I suggested that the ending in question came from an auxiliary which was ultimately a sort of COPULA. Goldenberg considers this an argument against the proto-Semitic origin "car on ne peut parler de catégorie de copule dans le sémitique commun." It is difficult enough to prove the existence of something in a reconstructed proto-language, but to prove the ABSENCE of something is absolutely impossible. Proto-Semitic may very well have had a copula that disappeared later in the present tense. Such developments are attested in languages (most spectacularly in French- and English-based creole or pidgin languages). Furthermore, the original verb could also have been an existential-locative verb 'there is' which could have evolved into a copula in some cases. In fact, Afroasiatic has such a verb, the existential *wnn* of Ancient Egyptian

and the locative verb of Bilin (Northern Agaw) *wắnna*. This *wn* could account for the alternation *u~n* in our endings: according to the environment one of the other phoneme survives. An
alternation *u~n* is found in the Western Gurage copula (*BSOAS* 35:455) and in the set of passive
formatives in Semitic (along with a *t* that is also found both as a copula and as a Main Verb-
Marker), which may be of a periphrastic origin with a copular auxiliary (see my forthcoming
article in *Mélanges de l'Université Saint-Joseph*). We thus find such a converging set of evi-
dences that counterarguments valid for only one of them should not be considered particularly
weighty.

The above was a set of replies to Goldenberg rather than a presentation of his article. It
should be pointed out that his contribution is very important, carefully built up and well-
documented, and it has proven very stimulating even to someone with whom Goldenberg expressed
disagreement and who is now expressing disagreement with him.

3.5. (Survey Article)
The Israeli Contribution to the Study of Neo-Syriac
By Iddo Avinery (Bar Ilan University)

3.5.1. THE NAME OF THE LANGUAGE

Prior to discussing the contribution of Israeli linguists concerning the publication of texts
in Neo-Syriac, a few words should be said about the name of this language. Neither the linguists
nor the speakers of this language have a clear and fixed name for it. Rivlin (1959) calls it
Lšon Targum 'Targum language', while Idelssohn (1913) gives it the name of *Aramit hadaša* 'Neo-
Aramaic' (although he mentions the name *Targum* used by historians and writers in the Middle
Ages to describe this language). *Neo-Syriac* or *Neo-Aramaic* is the accepted name in the
scientific literature, whereas *Kurdit* 'Kurdish' is the name mostly used by native speakers
of this language — in speech as well as in writing, see, for example, Binyamin and Baruch
(1973: front page and introduction) who write *bsafa kurdit caha brura unqiyya* 'in Kurdish
language, pure, clear and clean'. In a similar way *kurdi* 'Kurdish' (m.) is used by Avidani
(1959: front page). Polotsky (1960:180), after expressing his dissatisfaction with the name
"Targum Jews," writes: "As a matter of fact it is difficult to find an all-satisfactory name
for this language. Native speakers themselves call it just 'Kurdish', but in science language
this name is employed to denote the Iranian language of Muslim Kurds (*Kurmanği*). 'Eastern
Neo-Aramaic' is too long. 'Neo-Syriac', which is the most current name used in scientific
language, will hurt its Jewish speakers since *su:ra:ya* means for them 'Christian, uncircumcised'.
Kurdo-Aramit is short and adequate, but not quite correct from the Hebrew point of view." Later
on he uses in Hebrew the name *Kurdo-Aramit* 'Kurdo-Aramaic', but puts it between quotation marks.

It is evident that the adjective "Syriac" will not be accepted by Jewish speakers. Cohen
(1971:949), after citing such names as "the language of the Jews" and "Jabali" says: "It seems
that rabbinic scholars on rare occasions called this language Aramaic, as can be seen in two
manuscripts, one from the beginning of the eighteenth century, the other from the beginning of
the twentieth." He then remarks that the name "modern Syriac" is suitable to the Christian
dialects.

3.5.2. THE ORIGIN OF THE LANGUAGE

Opinions differ also about the origin of this language. Polotsky (1964:105) states that a near

relative of "Western" Syriac survives today in Torani and that the exclusive status of Syriac
as the only written language prevented the spoken Aramaic of "Assyria" (Mosul and its vicinity)
from being used in writing. He goes on to say that "it survives, however, in the Neo-East-
Aramaic ("Modern Syriac") dialects spoken today, or at least until very recently, by Christians
as well as Jews from Mosul to Persian Azerbaijan. On the other hand, the two varieties of
Babylonian Aramaic which were employed in writing in the Middle Ages, viz. the language of the
Babylonian Talmud and Mandaean, did not leave descendants." Cohen (1971:949) remarks that the
Christians who use this language consider Syriac the language from which their language evolved,
but he adds that there is no linguistic proof for this contention. He offers the assumption
that from historical-linguistic point of view the eastern dialects of Neo-Aramaic developed
from a language similar to Babylonian talmudic Aramaic and Mandaic, but that "there are no documents extant in this language since it was not used as a literary vehicle. Similarly, the
exact connection between eastern Neo-Aramaic and the Aramaic of the Babylonian Jews before
they began speaking Arabic is unknown." (cf. also Kutscher 1953:967-68 and 1972:24-25).

3.5.3.   TEXTS IN HEBREW TRANSCRIPTION

The contribution of Israel to the research of Neo-Syriac began with the publication of texts.
Already Idelssohn (1913) printed a tale in the dialect of Urmi Jews. It was given in Hebrew
transcription (and vocalization), followed by a translation. A short linguistic survey as
well as an explanation of the transcription are to be found in the introduction. It should be
noted that the letters *b, g, d, k, p, t* are not systematically printed with a *Dageš*. The
reason for this is that Idelssohn published the tale exactly as it was given to him by a sage
of Sablaġ, who assumedly composed this tale, has written it down and vocalized it. In this
transcription, therefore, the letter *b*, for example, may denote *b, v,* or even *bb*. Nevertheless one has to point out that the author of this tale used a descriptive system and not a
historical one, since he writes, for example, *yarxa* 'month' and not *yarḥa* etc. The tale itself
is a story about Rabbi Pinḥas, a holy man who used to help all sick people and all sterile
women, but whose wife herself was barren. The tale is written in the form of a rhymed prose,
describing the many miracles from God and ends with a prayer to a victory over Israel's
enemies.

The greatest contribution to recording texts in a Hebrew transcription, followed by translation and a commentary, was undoubtedly done and further encouraged by Rivlin (1959) who began
publishing stories in Neo-Syriac already in the twenties, including, *inter alia*, the story
of David and Goliath as well as many proverbs.[1] The importance of this text recording was
stressed by Polotsky (1960:181) in a rather emphatic manner. After pointing out the value of
the study of this language, since it enables us to watch the natural development of a language
which two thousand years back was the closest sister of the Hebrew language, he goes on to say:
"Were the relations between the Jewish dialects and the Christian ones examined in time, they
would have constituted a research capable of being a symbol of the combination between the
pure dialectological approach and the serious sociological one. The opportunity was missed...
What there is to be done must be done quickly. The time has not yet arrived when only one
single old man, last of his tribe, still remembers a few words and phrases of his fathers'
tongue... Professor Rivlin had long ago understood that here is an important task that an
Israeli orientalist must take on himself." Polotsky (1960:181) also mentions that the for-
getting of the language amongst the young generation is advancing in a frighteningly quick
manner. One should add here that already in the early fifties one could hear from young
people forms which were influenced by modern Hebrew, such as *misto:vivlu* 'they strolled'.

---

[1]A list of texts printed in a Hebrew transcription is given on page 70. One should here add
that many expressions and phrases in Neo-Syriac are to be found in the book written by
Brauer (1947), but their value is essentially folkloristic. See also the bibliography there
(Brauer, 1947: 295-306).

As was pointed out by Cohen (1971:951), it seems that epic poems on Biblical and Targum themes were first transcribed in Israel through the efforts of Joseph Joel Rivlin. Indeed, the book mentioned above contains various stories, beginning with Adam and Eve and ending with the construction of Jerusalem and the Temple. In the hundred pages introduction Rivlin surveys the poetry of the Jews of Kurdistan from many points of view, literary, historical and folkloristic. He praises (1959:8) the help of Polotsky in the vocalization and mentions the many notes of his which are printed in this book. These notes are of special interest: they deal mainly with etymology and morphology (and sometimes with phonetics too, as demonstrated by note 114 on page 138, where the root *xdm, ġdm* 'to serve' is discussed). In many cases Polotsky corrects the vocalization of the writers of these stories, e.g. page 230, note 5: on the form *ǧimʿalu* 'they gathered' he remarks "*ǧmaʿlu* certainly was intended." Cf. also pp. 153 (n. 4), 154 (n. 16), 156 (n. 31), 206 (n. 43), 242 (n. 121), 243 (n. 125 and 126).

Another collection of texts in Hebrew characters is to be found in a recently published, or rather photographed, book by Binyamin and Baruch (1973). It contains several *Piyyutim* which were translated and written down by Rabbi Yosef Binyamin of Zakho. They were copied by his son Shmuel Baruch, who added some prayers. Although the authors are from Zakho, a historical, or maybe dialectal, transcription is sometimes to be found, such as *pti:xe* 'open' instead of *psi:xe*, see Binyamin and Baruch (1973:151). This example is from the well known *ʿet šaʿarey racon* 'At the time when the ports of will'; in a manuscript which seems to be older than the one published by Baruch (kept by Avinery) this word is written "correctly" as *psi:xe*.

Regarding Biblical paraphrases see Sabar (1965).

UNPUBLISHED TEXTS in a Hebrew transcription are in the possession of several scholars in Isreal: a translation of Urmi and Zakho was transcribed over the period of thirty years through the efforts of Rivlin. Tales and prayers are also in the possession of Polotsky,[2] Cohen and Avinery. A manuscript which is vocalized better than most is in the hands of Cohen. It is written in the dialect of Sablaġ (new name: Mahabad), and is being investigated by Cohen who is comparing it to the spoken dialect.

3.5.4. TEXTS IN A PHONETIC TRANSCRIPTION

In a chronological order, texts were published by Garbel (1965), Polotsky (1967) and Avinery (1974 and 1975).

The texts published by Garbel (1965) are in the dialect of the Jews of Persian Azerbaijan. They cover the oral literature and as such are of value also to the folklorist. They include, *inter alia*, legends, folk stories, occupations of the Jews, the house and house works and poems. The transcription was done in a phonemic system. Of special interest is the English translation which includes a free translation as well as a literal one, illustrating the structure of Neo-Syriac. Kaddari (1966:503) stresses the importance of this presentation, saying "This combination of translations of two kinds is highly instructive for the linguist who studies it. Automatically he distinguishes between the different structures of the two languages. One example will suffice: 'Rise < upon your feet >, why have you lost courage <your-heart fell> ?' The details of these distinctions may be of interest not only to the scholar who studies this dialect, but to every one who takes interest in Semitic languages, since these patterns, or their like, are to be found in other Semitic languages, and their existence in this new linguistic material may often open our eyes."

The two excerpts published by Polotsky (1967a) are one in the dialect of Urmi and the other in the dialect of Zakho (this last one is in fact the essential material existing today in the dialect of the Jews of Zakho). The contents of the first text are hard and soft pronunciation,

---

[2]Some of these are already being printed in a Latin transliteration.

a letter, a story about the flight from Urmi in December 1914 (the narrator of this story
was picked up by a Russian soldier and put on an ammunition wagon) and a story entitled
"The Girl and the Fairy."   Polotsky (1967a:72-73) points out regarding this last story, "The
original publication, printed in the international phonetical alphabet [IPA] and here transcribed according to the system used in the preceding texts in order to facilitate its study,
is a most important source of information about the phonetics of the Urmi dialect."

The Zakho texts contain two episodes from a novel. They were dictated to Polotsky in 1947 by
Avraham Levy. The novel tells about a rich man who had three wives. Two of them started an
intrigue with the young gardener, were found out and expelled. Then the former gardener
has to go on a journey by himself. When he does not return, the two wives decide to search for
him. Here we read about the death of the first wife and about the adventures of the second
one.

As regards the transcription: apart from exceptional cases the stress generally is not marked
down, since it is almost always on the penultima. However, a certain grammatical knowledge is
required from the reader. For example, he has to know that in the phrase u'axö:n de: baxta
'and the brother of this woman' (Polotsky, 1967a:75) the stress of the first word is on the
last syllable, since 'axö:n here is in the construct state. Nevertheless the transcription
may be defined as narrow, rather than broad.

It is also of interest to remark on some changes in Polotsky's transcription as compared to
the one employed by him in texts which he printed in the fifties for the use of his disciples:
short *i* was replaced by *ə*. For example, instead of *riž* 'on' we find *rəž*; long vowels in a
last open syllable are specified. For example, instead of *gme:nxa* 'she looks' *game:nxa:* is
printed; in hendiadys expressions the copulative is in many cases affixed to the first word
with a hyphen. E.g. *ha:l u:qišta* 'the situation', 'the story', as well as *u:to:zu ʿijaj* 'and
dust', are replaced by *ha:l-u: qəšta:*, *u:tö:z-u: ʿəjaj*; the prefix *g* which denotes the present
tense is, in negative expressions, mostly attached to *la*. E.g. *la-kpa:yiš* 'does not remain'
is replaced by *lak pa:yiš*. Of these examples (Polotsky, 1967a:75-76) the last two are to be
found in their new form already in another version which was printed by Polotsky in the fifties
and read in his lectures.

As regards the glossary (Polotsky, 1967b) see the last chapter.

An everyday-life story in the dialect of Zakho was published by Avinery (1974). The subject
of this tale is somewhat unusual, since most texts in Neo-Syriac deal with folkloristic themes.
The contents of this story are about an invitation to a conference, which was organized for
the benefit of new immigrants to Israel. They were stopped by rain but finally succeeded to
arrive at the meeting place, only to be hampered by a guard for want of tickets. The story
ends with a philosophical conversation about the changes of social standings.

The transcription resembles in many details the one used by Polotsky (1967a,b), apart from
nonspecification of the length of vowels in a last open syllable. As regards stress: cases
in which the stress is not on the penultima were usually indicated, for example, (Avinery, 1974:
12) *múzi:ʿa* 'lost'; but not consecutively, e.g., (1974:13) *qqatli:walu:* 'they used to kill
them' was printed as *qqatli:walu:*. But unusual stress was always noted where it has no
grammatical conditioning, for instance on page 9 *'é:dison* 'Edison' (name of a cinema-house in
Jerusalem), and on p. 10, note 5 *si:nima* 'cinema'. The text is annotated, mostly with grammatical remarks, and followed by a Hebrew translation.

Another story in the dialect of Zakho was published by Avinery (1975), this one being a folkloristic tale. An insulted lion proves to his man-friend that words can hurt harder than
blows. There is a short introduction and bibliography followed by notes, mostly of grammatical nature, and a translation. The author remarks that the translation is sometimes verbal so
as to enable the reader to grasp the Neo-Syriac structure.

UNPUBLISHED TEXTS. The most important collection of unpublished texts is the one kept by Prof. Polotsky. It consists of many volumes which contain stories that were transcribed by him. Another collection, limited to the dialect of Zakho, is the one kept by Avinery. It contains, *inter alia,* the book of Jonah and a Neo-Syriac translation to the book of Henri Frei, *Le Livre des Deux Mille Phrases* (Genève, 1953). Avinery has also a collection of texts registered by tape recorder.[3] An ecclectic text in the dialect of the Jews of Nerwa and Amidya is to be found in a dissertation done by Y. Sabar. It is a detailed study of a homily on the *Parashah* of Bšallaḥ, as preserved in three seventeenth century manuscripts. The phonetic transcription is followed by a translation. Grammatical outlines of the Neo-Aramaic language of the manuscripts are included in the introduction.[4] A very brief grammatical survey will be found in the following paragraphs. It is mainly a study of some outlines of the dialect of the Jews of Zakho, with only a few remarks on other dialects.

3.5.5. PHONOLOGY

Cohen (1973:949-950) gives an interesting description out of which a few examples are here represented:

THE GLOTTAL STOP, $^{\circ}$, parallels three consonants of Ancient Aramaic, א, ע, ג. $^{\circ}$ from ע (or ג) is always retained, while the $^{\circ}$ from א is liable to disappear in certain situations: $^{\circ}ura$ 'road', $burxa$ 'on the road' as against $^{\circ}iṣra$ 'ten' and $b^{\circ}iṣra$ 'at ten'. This is a means to determine the etymological origin of a particular $^{\circ}$.

B, G, D, K, P, T which in Ancient Aramaic, as well as in Hebrew, had two variants each, have attained phonemic status for each of their variants.

As in Eastern Syriac, the phoneme פ is always pronounced p. In loanwords f is found. This is true concerning all Jewish dialects, while in most of the Christian dialects f is replaced by p. Other phonemes to be found in loanwords are $ḥ$, $ʿ$, $ǧ$, $č$, $ž$, v.

It should be noted that these rules and remarks were first said by Polotsky, either in his lectures at the Hebrew University or in his grammars.[5]

DOUBLING of consonants has been largely eliminated. Polotsky (see note 5) gives examples of substantives where this doubling was replaced by lengthening of the preceding vowel, e.g. $mayya$: 'water' > $ma:ya$; but in certain conditions and before voiced consonants this doubling was preserved, as $libba$ 'heart', $pümma$ 'mouth'. Polotsky also points out the transposition of the verbs ע"י into י"ע. E.g., the root כפף 'to bend' has become kyp. The same is true regarding verbs loaned from Arabic, e.g. $fya:ra$ 'to fly', Arabic $farra$.

THE PHONEME uy. Polotsky (1961:11) remarks that this phoneme was considered by the missionaries as a vulgar variant of $u:$. Thus, $nuyra$ 'fire' in the dialect of Urmi was changed to $nu:ra$. Polotsky (1961:12) points out that an examination of the phonemic status of uy would have shown that so far from being an "uneducated" free variant of $u:$, it is a separate phoneme.

---

[3] He has also in preparation a book which contains various texts in the Zakho dialect, annotated and followed by a translation and a dictionary.

[4] The above dissertation is kept at the Library of Linguistics at the Hebrew University of Jerusalem.

[5] A part of what was said by Polotsky in his lectures may be found in his yet unpublished grammars (the dialects of Zakho and Urmi). These two grammars are kept at the Library of Linguistics at the Hebrew University of Jerusalem.

When "note 5" will be later on mentioned in this study it will signify that whatever is cited in the name of Polotsky was either said by him (in his lectures etc.) or written by him in the above-mentioned grammars.

As was stated above, allophones of *b, g, d, k, p, t* no longer exist. Nevertheless, MORPHO-PHONEMIC RELATION can be found between *b* and *w* (which is the transposition of Old Syriac ܒ), *t* and *s* (OS ܢ) etc. The following examples were cited by Polotsky (n. 5): *kalba* 'dog', *kalwe* 'dogs'; *zwa:na* 'to buy', *mzabo:ne* 'to sell'; *mya:sa* 'to die', *mitle* 'he died'. The following correspondence was suggested by Avinery:[6] *qli:ba* 'turned over', versus *qli:wa* 'clean'.

VOICED AND VOICELESS ʾ. Polotsky (n. 5) mentions the form *ki:ʾe* 'he knows', where the prefix *k* (and not *g*) would suggest that the ʾ is voiceless and, on the other hand, the expression *ha:daǧ ʾuzle* 'so he did', where *ǧ* (and not *x*) seems to be influenced by a voiced ʾ.

SHORTENING OF A THIRD-LAST VOWEL. A long vowel in an antepenult open syllable becomes shorter before a long vowel. This rule of Polotsky (n. 5) was demonstrated by him in the following examples: *šqo:lu:n* 'take' (imp. pl.), versus *šqŭlu:le* 'take him'; *ma:ru:n* 'tell' (imp. pl.), vs. *măru:le* 'tell him'; *kšaqla:wa:* 'she would take', vs. *kšaqlăwa:le* 'she would take him'. Polotsky also adds the following limiting conditions: firstly, the third-last vowel must be *a:, e:,* or *o:* only; secondly, *e:* in verbs remains long. E.g., *hwe:le:la* 'was born to her'. This shows a difference of behavior between a vowel which belongs to the root and an infix.

Some remarks concerning the ARABIC ELEMENTS in Neo-Syriac were made by Avinery (see note 6):

After mentioning that Arabic ᶜ usually remains so in Neo-Syriac, Avinery gives some examples where Arabic ᶜ is represented by both ᶜ and ʾ: from Arabic *ṣnᶜ* we have both *saneʾta* 'work, profession' and *sanᶜatkar* 'expert workman' (this last form was reluctantly admitted by one informant, after having insisted on *ṣanʾatkar*. Later, she admitted that both form existed); Arabic ᶜǧb is represented both by *ʾǧible:le* 'it pleased him' and *mᶜo:ǧible* 'he wondered'; from Arabic ᶜwn there is *maʾo:ne* 'to help' and *ᶜya:na* 'to help' (usually in the expression *ʾi:la: ᶜa:yinnox* 'God help you.'); finally, the following opposition is to be found (from Arabic *rbᶜ*): *rubʾa:be* 'quarters of rupee, sixteen mils' vs. *rubᶜa:be* ' quarters'.

DOUBLING of consonants exists in "Aramaic" forms such as *mxasso:se* 'to renew'. All these forms belong to the second conjugation, *mC-*. Avinery adds the following verbs from the Arabic: *mzarro:re* 'to damage', *mᶜaddo:de* 'to wail, mourn', *mšatto:te* 'to disperse', *mᶜazzo:az* 'to honor', and *mxaffo:fe* 'lighten'. See also Polotsky (1967b:108): *mšakko:ke* 'to doubt, to be suspicious'. Regarding substantives he mentions these two oppositions, where the form with a doubled consonant is an "Arabic" one: *šaba:ka* (f.) 'net', vs. *šabba:ka* (f.) 'window'; *saha:ra* (m.) 'sorcerer', vs. *sahha:ra* (and also *sahha:re*) (f.) 'sorceress'.

THE AMBIGUITY OF THE SUFFIX *-e*. Arabic *ta:ʾ marbu:ta* may be rendered either as *a* or *e* (apart from the forms ending with *-ta, -ita* or *-at*). Thus, a form in the feminine singular may be identical with that of the plural. For example, *tifle* may signify either 'a (she) baby' or 'babies'.

THE DIPHTHONG *ay*. Usually it is monophthongized. However, the diphthong *ay* remains when it comes from Arabic *a:ʾi*. E.g., *qayma* 'list' (Ar. *qa:ʾima*), *tayfa* 'sect' (Ar. *ta:ʾifa*), and *fayda* 'use, advantage' (Ar. *fa:ʾida*).

Avinery hesitatingly remarks that in many cases "foreign" elements may be detected, either by the existence of phonemes which are found only in loanwords (such as ᶜ, *h, ǧ*) or by a behavior which does not correspond with the usual historical process (e.g. *qbille* 'he accepted'. Had this been the Aramaic root *qbl*, the form should have been **qulle*. The same applies to *nhible*

---

[6] In an unpublished work, entitled *The Arabic Elements in the Aramaic Language of the Jews of Zakho*. A part of this work was presented in 1967 to Prof. Polotsky as an M.A. thesis (it is kept at the Library of Oriental Studies at the Hebrew University of Jerusalem).

Regarding "foreign" elements see also Sabar (1974).

'he plundered', which should have been *nhu:le). Some kind of support to this idea may be found in Polotsky's words, when he remarks on the word ʾibmazivre:na (here transliterated from the Hebrew) 'I shall turn': "Of a Kurdish origin, as the v shows." (Rivlin, 1959:244, n. 142).

3.5.6. MORPHOLOGY AND SYNTAX

A short morphological description of the dialect of Zakho is given by Cohen (1971:950). He mentions that in the PLURAL there is no differentiation of gender in adjectives, pronouns, or the verb. The examples given by him are: go:ra sqi:la 'a handsome man', baxta sqilta 'a beautiful woman', gu:re sqi:le 'handsome men', and baxta:sa sqi:le.

Concerning the VERB Cohen points out that it differs radically from Ancient Aramaic both in form and in content. The form ša:qil, which was the active participle in Ancient Aramaic, is a subjunctive. The present is formed by prefixing g/k to ša:qil, e.g., gza:mir 'he plays'. The form šqi:l, passive participle in Ancient Aramaic is the basis of the past and the recipient of the action: šqille 'he took', šqi:la:le 'he took her' etc. Concerning the šqi:l form see also Kutscher (1953:968) who compares it to   'I heard' (from 'it was heard to/by me') in the Babylonian Talmud.

One should here add that all the grammatical observations made above, as well as all those that are to follow, were first pointed out by Polotsky (n. 5).

Cohen (1971:950) also gives a short survey about the NEW COMPOUND TENSES in Neo-Syriac. The present continuous, for example is formed by the infinitive šqa:la (bi usually precedes the infinitive of the first conjugation) plus the copula. Thus, bišqa:la: le: 'he is taking'. A most profound description of the tense-system in NS is given by Polotsky (1961:20-23). He argues with Nöldeke and says: "Our admiration for Nöldeke's grammar must not prevent us from realizing that in the light of the material at our disposal some of his views, not only on small matters of detail, stand in need of thorough revision. This applies in particular to his treatment of the tenses...". He later points out that Nöldeke was inclined to doubt the genuineness of phrasal verb-forms which failed to conform to his notions of linguistic efficiency. The present continuous is considered by Nöldeke as the only worthwhile addition to the tense-system, but is nevertheless allowed to pass as "nicht eben weitläufig."

As regards the TENSE-SYSTEM of the dialect of Sabalg̣, the following observation was made by Cohen. The perfect in this dialect is formed in two ways: for intransitive verbs we have zi:lin (= zi:l + in) 'I have gone', while for transitive verbs one finds xilte:la (xilta + i:la) 'she has eaten', with two different sets of subject-markers.

THE POSSESSIVE SUFFIX -an, -e:ni. Polotsky (1961: 19) remarks that this suffix of 1st pers. pl. has a specific distinction between its two forms, at any rate as far as regards the Urmi dialect: the possessors denoted by the suffix -enij are the family or the village community to which the speaker belongs. He adds that in the dialect of Zakho, on the contrary, -an and e:ni seem to be free variants. In this connection Avinery (1974: 12) cites an informant who, after hearing the form zille:ni: 'we went', remarked: "Boys and girls say zille:ni, se:le:ni 'we came'." (instead of zillan, se:lan)

THE SUFFIX OF THE PLURAL -a:sa, -(a)wa:sa. Avinery (n.6) remarks that this suffix of Old Syriac is added also to substantives which are derived from Arabic, and even masculine ones. E.g. g̣ula:ma 'servant', pl. g̣ulam(w)a:sa; ʿag̣ab 'wonder', pl. ʿag̣ābwa:sa; ʾe:ra 'male organ', pl. ʾerawa:sa. In the feminine there are: xe:ma 'tent', pl. xe:ma:sa; qaḥba 'whore', pl. qaḥba:sa.

THE STATUS CONSTRUCTUS. Cohen (1971:950) observes that the new st. const. is formed by adding the suffix -it to the noun base. He cites the example baxta 'a woman', baxtit axo:na 'the brother's wife'. However, not all nouns have a construct state, as shown by Polotsky (n. 5), who pointed out that there is re:š from re:ša 'head' but not du:k from du:ka 'place'. The reason for this is that nouns ending by -V:Ca can be in the construct state if their last consonant is a continuant (s, $\check{s}$, z, $\check{z}$, x, g) or a liquid (l, m, n, r). Some exceptions: *brat* 'the daughter of'; *lya:p* 'the study of' (*b²i:nitit lya:p li:ša:ne* 'with the intention of studying languages').

POSSESSIVE INFLECTION (*Cmidut*). Polotsky (n. 5) treats the problem of noun inflection, whether by possessive pronouns suffixed to the nouns or by *d-*, *di:d-* plus the possessive pronouns. He mentions the form *baxti* 'my wife' as "strong *cmidut*" and adds that members of the body are thus inflected. Avinery (n. 6) cites the following examples: *ǧwa:b di:de* 'his answer', as against *ǧwa:bi* 'my answer'; and the French expression *J'ai mal à l'estomac* which was translated in two ways, *maᶜde: di:di: gmar²a:* 'my stomach aches' as well as *maᶜdi we:la qlibta* 'my stomach is turned upside down'.

3.5.7. LEXICON

Glossaries of Neo-Syriac were published by Garbel (1965) and Polotsky (1967b).

Garbel's glossary deals with the dialect of Persian Azerbaijan. As pointed out by Kaddari (1966:504) this is not just a dictionary of words, but rather a collection of linguistic units which do not have a grammatical significance. These so-called "lexemes" can be: verbal-root-morphemes, verbal stems, and free and bound lexemes. Sometimes the origin of the lexeme is noted. A bibliographical list of dictionaries is also given.

Polotsky's glossaries deal with the dialects of Urmi and Zakho. They are arranged in the order of a Latin alphabet. An innovation in the glossary of Zakho is the introduction of s_2 and z_2, in which denote old   and   respectively. For example, *²wa:z₂a* 'to do', *²i:s₂a:ya* 'to come', as against *²i:za:la* 'to go', *msa:ya* 'to wash'.

There is a clear distinction between the arrangement of verbs and nouns: whereas verbs are arranged according to their roots, nouns are given in the order of their consonants only. For example, we find *qya:ma* 'to rise' under *qym*, *twa:ra* 'to break' under *twr*; but *be:sa* 'house' is found under *bs*, *li:ša:na* 'tongue' under *lšn*, and *šu:la* 'work' under *šl*.

AN UNPUBLISHED DICTIONARY. A dictionary of the Zakho dialect is in preparation at the Department of Hebrew and Semitic Languages at Bar-Ilan University. It is done under the direction of Avinery, and sponsored by the research committee of the university.

Finally, on the importance of Neo-Syriac lexicography one should be referred to Kutscher (1953: 968; 1961:20,100; and 1972:24-25) who, *inter alia*, points out the influence of Neo-Syriac on Modern Hebrew.

3.5.8. REFERENCES

Avidani, A.S.B.
   1959 *Seder Haggada shel Pesaḥ* [The Ritual of Passover] (Jerusalem: Avidani).

Avinery, Iddo
   1974 "Sipur baniv ha²arami shel yehudey Zaxo" [A Tale in the Aramaic Dialect of the Jews
        of Zakho], *Enoch Yalon Memorial Volume*, ed. by M.Z. Kaddari (Ramat-Gan: Bar-Ilan
        University), 8-16.

   1975 "A Text in Neo-Syriac," *Journal of the American Oriental Society*

Binyamin, Yosef and Baruch, Shmuel
   1973 (erroneously printed 1873) *Sefer taᶜamey hamicvot* [The Book of the Reasons of
        Commandments] (Jerusalem).

Brauer, E.
   1947 *Yehudey Kurdistan* [The Jews of Kurdistan] (Jerusalem: The Israeli Institute of
        Folklore and Ethnology).

Cohen, David
    1971 "Neo-Aramaic," *Encyclopaedia Judaica* 6 (Jerusalem), 948-951.

Garbel, I.
    1965 *The Jewish Neo-Aramaic Dialect of Persian Azerbaijan* (The Hague: Mouton).

Idelssohn, Avraham Cvi
    1913 "Sipurim balašon haʾaramit hahadaša" [Stories in the Neo-Aramaic Language],
          Haschiloah 29, 121-130, 240-25-, 319-327, 466-474, 552-561.

Kaddari, M.Z.
    1966 Review of *The Jewish Neo-Aramaic Dialect of Persian Azerbaijan* by I. Garbel, *Kiryat
          Sefer* 41, 499-504.

Kutscher, Yechezkel
    1953 "Aramit" [Aramaic], *The Hebrew Encyclopedia* 5 (Jerusalem and Tel-Aviv: Massada),
          959-969.

    1961 *Milim vetoldoteyhen* [Words and their History] (Jerusalem: Kiryat Sepher).

    1972 *ʾerxey hamilon hehadaš lesifrut hazal* [Words in the New Dictionary of Talmudic
          Literature] 1, ed. by Yechezkel Kutscher (Ramat-Gan: Bar-Ilan University).

Polotsky, Hans Jakob
    1960 "'Yehudey hatargum' ulšonam" [The 'Targum Jews' and their Language] *Gesher* 6, 180-181.

    1961 "Studies in Modern Syriac," *Journal of Semitic Studies* 6, 1-32.[7]

    1962 Review of *Zwei russische Novellen in neusyrischer Übersetzung und Lateinschrift* by
          J. Friedrich, *Orientalia* 31, 273-283.

    1964 "Semitics," *The World History of the Jewish People* (Tel-Aviv: Massadah), 99-111,
          357-358.

    1967a "Eastern Neo-aramaic: Urmi and Zakho," *An Aramaic Handbook* II/1, ed. by Franz
          Rosenthal (Wiesbaden: Otto Harrassowitz), 69-77.

    1967b "Eastern Neo-Aramaic," *An Aramaic Handbook* II/2, ed. by Franz Rosenthal (Wiesbaden:
          Otto Harrassowitz), 97-111.

Rivlin, Yoṣef Yoel
    1959 *Sirat yehudey hatargum* [Poetry of the *Targum* Jews] (Jerusalem: The Bialik Institute).

Sabar, Yona
    1965 "Tafsirim lamikra ufiyutim bilšonam haʾaramit šel yehudey kurdistan" [Paraphrases
          of the Bible and Hymns in the Neo-Aramaic of the Jews of Kurdistan], *Sefunot* 10,
          337-412.

    1974 "Haysodot haᶜivriyim baniv haʾarami šel yehudey zaxo bkurdistan" [The Hebrew Elements
          in the Neo-Aramaic dialect of the Jews of Zakho], *Lešonenu* 38, 206-219.

---

[7] It also contains an important bibliography. A fuller bibliography was printed by Polotsky in the fifties (in a stencil form) and used by his students.

3.6.   V.S. XRAKOVSKIY, *Očerki po obščemu i arabskomu sintaksisu*, Moscow, 1973.
     By T.M. JOHNSTONE (School of Oriental and African Studies, The University of London).

In this book of some 290 pages the first three chapters (pp. 5-121) deal with general linguistic problems, and the remaining three chapters with specific linguistic questions of Arabic syntax.

The first of the general chapters deals with transformational and derivational relationships, the second with formal and semantic features of paradigmatic derivation and the third with the correlation of the formal, syntactic and linear structure of the sentence. The analysis in this section of the book prepares the ground for the author's later chapters on Arabic.

The final three chapters of the book deal with certain classes of operators. Chapter 4 deals with what the author calls "causative verbs," which however are semantically and not formally causative (viz. not of the ʾafʿala theme). The verbs discussed in fact are those which have a subordinating function, such as ʾaḏina 'to allow', ʾamara 'to order', jaʿala 'to make' etc. The analysis of the function of this class of verbs as operators within the sentence is one of considerable interest for Arabists.

The following chapter deals with what the writer calls "operator verbs of subjective modality." The modal verbs whose function is studied and analyzed are the verbs of wishing, hoping, fearing, deciding and thinking, etc., as well as the verbs of being able.

The last chapter deals with what are called "operator phase verbs." The writer makes clear what he means by "phase verbs" by defining them as ʾaxawātu kāna and "ʾafʿālu š-šurū", namely verbs of being and becoming, and verbs of beginning. In his text however he includes also verbs of continuing, remaining and finishing (such as baqiya, istamarra and ʾanhā).

The analysis is fairly detailed throughout but the argumentation does not seem to depend so entirely on detail that the author could not have given a final chapter in which he sums up.

Some account is taken in this book of the work of Western linguists though the references in the bibliography seem to be rather random, and only one of Chomsky's publications is listed.

3.7.   HAYON, HEHIEL, *Relativization in Hebrew*.   (Janua Linguarum, Series Practica, 189), The Hague: Mouton, 1973, 240 pp.
     By TALMY GIVÓN (University of California, Los Angeles)

This book is unique both in the scope of its coverage (very wide) and its relatively up-to-date approach to analysis (Chomsky '65 Transformational), and for those two reasons alone it is of great value. It touches, in one manner or another, most major bases in the field of Hebrew relativization, as well as a number of related minor ones. And it is clearly and lucidly written, making the data easily accessible to readers with divergent interests. This inherent clarity and accessibility also make it possible for the reader to appreciate the exact points where the particular methodological/theoretical strictures adopted by the author begin to undermine the usefulness of his enterprise.

The book covers with reasonable detail the following aspects of the topic: Relativization of clauses with verbal predicates, relativization of clauses with non-verbal (copular) predicates, independent (or "headless") relative clauses, the relative markers ("subordinators"), word order in main and relative clauses, as well as a number of so-called residual problems. There is a great number of interesting insights scattered along the various chapters, and on the whole it is a thorough introduction to the subject, though one may occasionally wish to quarrel with the way the various sub-areas have been sequenced relative to each other. The comments that I will make below are thus not intended to detract in any way from this book's worth, but rather to point out the areas in which the various *a priori* methodological positions adopted by the author seem to have encroached upon the effectiveness of his product, and in some cases, also to mask his own— inherently often valid— intuitions.

1. DIACHRONY AND THE HEBREW MULTI-DIALECTISM.

The author adopts whole-heartedly de Saussure's strictures concerning the separation of diachronic from synchronic study, and chastises earlier Hebrew grammarians who failed to do likewise. With respect to the role of Biblical and Mishnaic form/structures in Modern Hebrew, he rather facilely assumes that some of them were incorporated into "the language." Though in a late chapter he comes close to admitting that the problem of syntactic variation in Modern Hebrew tends to defy one's ability to contend with it within the bounds of "the same" synchronic grammar, the book on the whole remains full to the brim of rather controversial data. What the author occasionally alludes to as "literary style" is, to my mind, not simply a "style" but rather, quite obviously, another DIALECT level of Hebrew. Indeed, most native speakers of Modern Hebrew, it seems to me, are multi-dialectal in the extreme. But this does not necessarily make the situation as unique as the author would like us to believe. The co-existence of CONFLICTING GRAMMARS with the "competence" of the very same speaker is the rule, not the exception, in language. Those "conflicting grammars" may stratify on age, education, social, literary and other gradients. But the pretense that ANY speaker has only one, internally-consistent grammar is at best a necessary METHODOLOGICAL convenience, to be adopted at the beginning of the investigation, rather than a dogma to be adhered to forever. The Saussurean strictures thus make the linguist which abides by them, ultimately, incapable of dealing with the most pervasive feature of language, namely that it is always in the middle of change, and that conflicting, parallel, co-existing grammars are the name of the game, rather than an arcane exception peculiar to languages which were dead and later revived.

In the case of Hebrew, the problem is obviously compounded by the traditional attitude which refused to recognise the conflicting nature of the variant codes which the speaker is capable of manipulating. In this sense the author is quite correct in taking the traditionalist to task. But his own admission of the enormity of the "stylistic variation" found in the "competence" of native speakers, ought to have given him pause for further reflection. Thus, to my mind "legitimate" examples cited by the author to illustrate his "competence", are in numerous cases NOT IN THE SAME DIALECT, i.e. not illustrative of the same grammar. And a great number of those are so artificial to my ear, as to suggest that they are not within ANY competence of native speakers — though of course they are still perfectly interpretable/intelligible.

2. PERFORMANCE AND COMPETENCE.

The author adopts eagerly Chomsky's methodological stricture, pegging the goal of the grammar as a device characterising what the speaker "knows" rather than how he "utilizes" his knowledge. Were Modern Hebrew less full of multi-dialectism and "stylistic variation," this approach would have gone the same distance it has gone for other languages, where reasonably useful descriptions — up to a certain depth — can be obtained without recourse to textual frequencies and relative contextual distributions. Given the situation in Modern Hebrew, however, one finds numerous examples for which the author claims membership in his competence (or "idiolect"), to be of rather dubious status. Further, in a number of cases the variability, though perhaps initially reflecting differences between Biblical, Mishnaic and Modern idiom, has already assumed other valuations, most commonly with respect to DISCOURSE STRUCTURE. Let me cite one brief example. In his discussion of "basic" word order in Hebrew, Hayon cites, in addition to the preferred SVO, a number of other possible orders (pp. 198-199):

(6.2) *david 'axal 'et habanana*   (SVO)   'David ate the banana'

(6.3) *'axal david 'et habanana*   (VSO)

    (6.4) *'et habanana axal david*   (OVS)

    (6.5) *'et habanana david 'axal*   (OSV)

    (6.6) **david 'et habanana 'axal*   (SOV)

    (6.7) **'axal 'et habanana david*   (VOS)

With respect to these variants, one could make the following observations: (6.3) is absolutely out in the "street dialect," may be found only in some literary styles, and I, for once, cannot find a context in which I could ever use it. Though as Hayon points out later, it is an OK order in object relative clauses. (6.4) is OK only in topicalized & contrastive contexts, i.e. where 'banana' is topic-shifted to the left and *david* gets a contrastive stress, as against possible others who might have eaten the banana but didn't; (6.5) is only OK with a contrastive stress on the verb *'axal* 'ate', i.e. in contrast to other things David may have done with the banana but didn't; (6.6) is equally starred for me as for Hayon, but also equally starred for me as (6.3). That is, I cannot imagine either a "stylistic" or a discourse context in which I'd be caught dead using this order; (6.7), on the other hand, the VOS order, is actually alive and well in one major discourse environment, i.e. DISCOURSE INITIAL (Hetzron's (1971) PRESENTATIVE function). The actual example is of course pragmatically silly, but consider the equivalent:

    ba' 'elay 'ish 'exad 'etmol baboker ve'amar....

    V   O   S

    'A man came to me yesterday morning and said...'

And this is NOT a stylistic device within a literary dialect, but rather quite common in the "street dialect" to which I attempt, whenever feasible, to refer my acceptability judgements. In fact, this device of fronting the verb (predicate) is a universal device, as Hetzron (1971) has shown. Now, it is perfectly true that the author could have made the very same observations by introspecting, i.e. consulting his own idiolect or "competence." However, these are normally the types of observations about language which become manifest only when the linguist begins to count the actual text distribution of various "possible" forms. And that is precisely what strict adherence to the (initially useful) Chomskian orthodoxy, of studying "competence" in isolation from "performance," tends to discourage among linguists.

In a rather curious fashion, Hayon is ultimately a victim of the very same fault he finds in the traditional approach: He has admitted the "diachronic" variants into the "competence" of the speaker of Modern Hebrew, and he is thus committed to describe them as "generated" by the same grammar. Although this is conveniently termed "synchronic" rather than "panchronic," the problem remains the same — the linguist's reluctance to wrestle with the exact nature of the socio-educational-literary-discourse factors which condition the distribution of these "stylistic variants" in the speech of the native speaker.

3. THE FORMAL STRICTURES.

Here I wish to comment on two separate issues. One is basically trivial: Much space in this book is accorded to elaborate PS trees and sequenced T-rules, with various intermediates that are not motivated by anything in the data, but rather by formalism-internal considerations. While it is true that this type of description was for a long time in vogue and to some extent still is (at least for the purpose of writing a dissertation), it nevertheless adds nothing to our knowledge of relativization in general and relativization in Hebrew in particular. This is by no means a damning criticism, especially since I myself have in the past indulged in the same type of practices. In retrospect, however, it seems to me that the inordinate amount of space accorded to those highly formalistic, largely data-free manipulations, simply takes away time from the real purpose of what most of us would like to spend our print-time on, namely the exposition of facts about language(s) and the types of underlying generalizations illuminated by those facts.

A good example of how the adherence to a "universal" formal solution may lead to a cavalier disregard of the actual language-specific facts, may be found in Hayon's treatment of non-verbal ("copular") predicates in Hebrew. Essentially, the copula in Hebrew is seldom found in the present tense, but it is obligatory in past and future tenses, as well as in a number of other environments. Hayon's solution is of course one of the two obvious formalisms available within Transformational Grammar: Consider the copula a "meaning free" element, don't stipulate it in the PS rules, then insert it transformationally in a range of environments, which if one computes properly, turn out to be the majority of the sentential types in the language. What has been gained from this is precious little, all of it of formal, "economy" nature, and very little of it reflecting the actual surface facts of Hebrew syntax. Even the small "universality" gain, for which Hayon cites Bach (1967), is rather dubious. One of the most universal facts about languages, as one studies their variant surface typologies, is the consistency of separation between stative and active predication. And in one guise or another, as "semantic" representation of "state," "identity," "property" or "location," or as overt syntactic representation of all or some of those, languages tend to eventually develop some type of a "copular" phenomenon. To claim that it is merely a "tense/aspect carrier" in no way detracts from the amazing universality of the differential treatment which languages tend to accord to active and stative predication. Thus, while the tendency toward a "universal" formalism in syntax quite often simply tends to obscure the facts of a particular language, adherence to a PARTICULAR "universal" claim may, on occasion, tend to be not quite universal.

4. INTERNALLY MOTIVATED VS. CONTACT-MOTIVATED CHANGE.

On p. 214 the author makes a statement that one tends to hear often concerning Hebrew, namely that "...there is a strong influence of non-Semitic languages on the structure of Hebrew..." and that this influence is also felt in the area of word order. The author makes absolutely no attempt to substantiate this claim, and I'd like to contend that this claim about Modern Hebrew is totally unsubstantiated. The variant-order types exhibited currently in the "street dialect" of Modern Hebrew, and in particular those which function to differentiate various discourse contexts, are all attested in Biblical and Mishnaic Hebrew. Further, one could show that the bulk of the change from a largely VSO syntax of Early Biblical Hebrew to the currently dominant SVO of modern Hebrew (again the "street dialect"), has been virtually completed in Mishnaic Hebrew, and in fact even in Late Biblical Hebrew. So that the VSO → SVO shift could by no stretch of the imagination be ascribed to contact. But beyond this there's a much more serious question. In Indo-European, Malayo-Polynesian, Semitic and other language families one finds a typologically distinct drift from a certain type of VSO syntax toward SVO. The main driving force behind this change seems to be the universal tendency to (a) make the AGENT the subject, and (b) move TOPICAL material to sentence initial positions (see extensive discussion in Hetzron, 1971, Keenan, 1974, Vennemann, 1973, Givón, 1974). And languages which are in the midst of undergoing this type of change, seem to exhibit (i) many survivals of VSO order, and (ii) a great degree of word-order freedom, which usually tends to distribute along discourse-environment functions. To my knowledge, there's nothing in the syntax of Modern Hebrew to suggest that it is anything but a typical example of these universal tendencies.

REFERENCES

Bach, E. (1967) "*Have* and *be* in English syntax," *Language*, 43:462-485)

Givón, T. (1974) "Topic, pronoun and grammatical agreement," presented at the CONFERENCE ON SUBJECT AND TOPIC, UCSB, March 8-9, 1975

Hetzron, R. (1971) "Presentative function and presentative movement," in *Studies in African Linguistics*, supplement #2

Keenan, E. (1974) "Toward a universal definition of 'subject of'," presented at the CONFERENCE ON SUBJECT AND TOPIC, UCSB, March 8-9, 1975

Vennemann, T. (1973) "Topics, subjects and word-order: From SXV to SVX via TVX," *First International Congress of Historical Linguistics*, Edinburgh, September 1973 (ms)

3.8. *Linguistics* **120 (Jan 15, 1974), published by Mouton & Co.**
   By MICHEL MASSON (C.N.R.S., Paris)

The 120th issue of *Linguistics* is entirely devoted to sociolinguistic problems in Israel. In an introductory article (9-13), Prof. J. FISHMAN indicates that language planning is the most salient sociological fact in that country (its national language resulting from a language planning process) but that, curiously enough, it has never aroused scholarly attention. After defining two types of language planning (STATUS and CORPUS planning), he sketches the main lines of a program of study of this process with special reference to the Israel reality and emphasizes the fact that this problem is a subdivision within the sociology of language and its study must be undertaken in connection with the sociology of language as a whole.

One article is devoted to the description of the Academy, the official Israeli language-planning body; two studies deal with the impact of language planning in the field of chemistry and automotive vocabulary and another one with the unplanned part of Modern Hebrew, viz. slang. Some pages deal with the opinions of the Hebrew-speaking public about their own language.

"The Academy of the Hebrew Language": by JACK FELLMAN (95-103)

The author delineates the genesis of the Academy (the creation of a Council, Ben Yehuda's work and difficulties, the transformation of the Council into an Academy with a legal status in 1954), its composition, its way of working and its accomplishments.

Until now, the Academy's attention was mostly focused upon lexical creation—an urgent necessity in the case of a language suffering from a considerable shortage of words both in technical and every-day areas. According to the author, the Academy's work has generally been successful (in fact, we think this should be proved; cf. the following articles) and it constitutes a model for Academies of other developing languages, but it will have to avoid ossification, to improve its diffusion media and handle the problems of style and grammar— though, he goes on, it is not certain whether an Academy can handle such problems. This leads us to ask: now that the lexical shortage has been overcome, is the Academy not tending to become a useless body, like its French counterpart?

"The prediction of success in language planning: the case of chemists in Israel": by Jack E. HOFMAN (36-65).

This is a survey of the attitudes of seventy-five Israeli chemists toward language and social issues, of their knowledge and background in languages, the information they possess on language planning.

"Official Hebrew terms for parts of the car: a study of knowledge, usage and attitudes": by YAFA ALLONI-FAINBERG (67-94).

Israeli drivers were asked whether they knew and used 25 innovated Hebrew terms for parts of the car, selected so as to study the possible importance of word length, homonymy, foreign origin, and the coexistence of established alternate terms in popular use. The last two factors seem to be of considerable importance. The mass media appear to have been ineffective in disseminating these words.

"A study of the longevity of Hebrew slang": by ILANA KORNBLUETH and SARAH AYNOR (15-37).

Native Israelis, about 18-21 years old (127 high school students and 72 soldiers) were presented with a list of 120 usual slang words or phrases falling into four equal groups according to their origin: Arabic, Yiddish, Hebrew, English.

To establish how far and why they were living elements for them or not, the respondents were asked if they understood them, had heard or used them.

It appears that 1) the most alive forms are generally Hebrew and English, Arabic coming next followed by Yiddish; now, Hebrew is the respondents' language. English the language they know best: therefore, there is probably a link between the longevity of forms and the knowledge of the language of origin of these forms. 2) Addresses and exclamations were claimed to be used more extensively than other slang expressions. 3) Words rather than phrases were claimed to be more frequently used. 4) At least, half of the population claimed to have recently and frequently used single words of Hebrew origin.

This most instructive inquiry, which comprises a stimulating piece of self-criticism, might be questioned on one point: do the quoted Hebrew and English words or phrases always belong to slang and to the same sort of slang as the Arabic and Yiddish ones?

"Attitudes and opinions of Israeli teachers and students about aspects of Modern Hebrew": by F. SECKBACH (105-124).

To know what the Israelis think of Modern Hebrew, F. Seckbach presented a questionnaire to Hebrew-speaking Israelis divided into two groups: the former, that of the "judges" composed of Israelis notoriously interested in Hebrew as writers or linguists; the latter was constituted of students and teachers; the purpose was to examine whether they were as interested in Hebrew as the judges. The questions dealt with Hebrew experts, good Hebrew dictionnaries, good modern Hebrew grammars, authors and journalists using good Hebrew, social or regional dialects of Israeli Hebrew, groups speaking poor Hebrew or writing bad Hebrew, word-naming for Hebrew Grammar, Chemistry and Civics.

It appears that the latter group, especially the students, is comparatively little interested in Hebrew—considerably less than the elders would certainly have been, and this probably means that the speakers are conscious that their language has acquired a well-assured situation

Let us remind the authors that their articles can be of interest even for linguists who do not know Hebrew: why did they not consistently translate all the quoted items? But this is a minor piece of criticism. On the whole, this volume provides information on a subject practically untouched until now and it is presented in a serious, clear, and well-documented way. For the benefit of sociolinguistics, we can only hope that it will be followed by further similar studies.

4. ANCIENT EGYPTIAN

4.1. SHISHA–HALÉVY, ARIEL, "Apodotic EFSŌTEM: a hitherto unnoticed late Coptic tripartite pattern conjugation-form and its diachronic perspective," *Le Muséon* 86: 455-466 (1973).
By JOHN CALLENDER (University of California, Los Angeles)

In this article the author discusses a verbal form used exclusively in the apodoses of conditional sentences in certain documents in Sahidic Coptic that were written in the Theban area. He concludes that this form is non-standard, and hence not to be related paradigmatically to standard Sahidic forms. The author derives this form diachronically from a Late-Egyptian form *iw.f ḥr sḏm* '(if...), then he will hear' which is used in the same way.

The first problem encountered is that of identificaiton. A number of separate verb forms with different negations and different syntactic uses, show the same form *efsōtm*:

2nd Present: e-f-$s\bar{o}tm$ 'the way he hears is...' < LE i-$ir.f$ $s\underline{d}m$,
                    neg. e-f-tm-$s\bar{o}tm$ 'the way he hears is not...'

circumstantial: e-f-$s\bar{o}tm$ 'while he hears' < LE $iw.f$ hr $s\underline{d}m$,
                    neg. e-n-f-$s\bar{o}tem$ an 'while he does not hear'

The second present is a main clause form, whereas the circumstantial is a dependent clause form.
The form that the author is examining is a main clause form, but unlike the second present, or
the circumstantial, it can affix its direct object to the verbal base, i.e. e-f-$s\bar{o}tm$-s 'he
hears it'. Thus, neither by meaning or syntax can this new form $efs\bar{o}tem$ be identified with
either of the above. However, there is an additional tense, that seems to be sporadically
written the same as the form in question:

3rd Future: e-f-e-$s\bar{o}tm$ (late var. e-f-$s\bar{o}tm$) 'he will hear; may he hear' <
                    LE $iw.t.r.s\underline{d}m$,
                    neg. nne-f-$s\bar{o}tem$ 'he will not hear'

Although like the form under discussion, the Third Future admits a direct object affixed
directly to the verbal stem, the author rejects identifying his form as a variant of the Third
Future. The argumentation is unclear, but to the extent I can make it out, two reasons are
considered to militate against identifying it with the Third Future:

(1) Writings of the Third Future as e-f-$s\bar{o}tm$ are almost always phonologically
     conditioned (although he mentions one counterexample)

(2) Examples of the Third Future in these Theban documents are always MODAL (= non-
     main clause ???) and are rare

The counterexample ShT 368 *pnoute efjōōk ebol mpekouōs* 'God will send you forth and you did
not wish it' is considered by the author to be a Third Future written like the form in question.
This one counterexample, however, is not only non-conditioned, either phonologically or syntactically, but is also non-modal, in the meaning non-main clause, although one might argue that
it is modal in the sense that it does not refer specifically to a point in time. If so then
this form is extra-temporal, just like the form that the author is studying, and one would
think this would be one reason for identifying these forms as Third Futures. Thus one seems
to be left with only the claim that Third Futures are statistically rare in Theban Sahidic. If
these forms turn out to be Third Futures, we would, of course, have more. In any case, it seems
to me that the identification of these apodosis forms with Third Future forms represents the
crux of the matter, and the argumentation against such an identification is too sketchy to
be convincing. The issue is obscured by the author by coupling the identification of his form
with a Third Future with the implausible suggestion by Till that the forms be considered
variants of the First Perfect (a-f-$s\bar{o}tm$), which in the context of the discussion serves as a
red herring.

The author wishes to derive this form synchronically from an apodosis form attested in Late
Egyptian, written $iw.f$ hr $s\underline{d}m$. The existence of this form is disputed, since the preposition
hr had ceased to be pronounced in verbal constructions of this sort, and as a consequence is
often written by scribes in constructions where it had no place being, etymologically. This is
to say, these apodosis $iw.f$ hr $s\underline{d}m$ forms could be writings of the Third Future ($iw.f$ (r) $s\underline{d}m$),
since the r in such forms is often not written. This issue, therefore, also remains moot.

This article, therefore, raises a number of important issues, and should be consulted by any-
one interested in Coptic grammar and dialectology. The reader must be prepared, however, to
get through the somewhat idiosyncratic and over-technical prose of the Polotsky-Groll school.

5. CUSHITIC

5.1. HETZRON, ROBERT, "An archaism in the Cushitic verbal conjugation," in *IV Congresso Internazionale di Studi Etiopici (Roma, 10-15 aprile 1972)*, Tomo II, (Sezione Linguistica; Problemi Attuali di Scienza e di Cultura, 191). Rome: Accademia Nazionale dei Lincei, 1974, pp. 275-281.

By R.J. HAYWARD (School of Oriental and African Studies, London)

This is a most stimulating paper. In tackling a question which initially promises to be of syntactic and typological interest to Cushiticists, an answer emerges which affords a very much clearer understanding of genetic relations between Semitic and Cushitic as reflected in their verbal morphology.

In languages as widely separated as Somali and Southern Agaw conjugations of the verbal paradigm with only three (S. Agaw) or four (Somali) distinct forms occur alongside conjugations with six. In both languages one form serves for Sg./Pl. 2 and Sg.masc./Pl. 3 (Sg.fem. 3 too in S. Agaw). Syntactically these "impoverished conjugation" forms function in subordinate clauses. Insofar as the neutralisation of person, number and gender distinctions is only partial[1] the question as to why it should have happened at all arises. The merging of Sg./Pl. 2/3 forms which results from the absence of the characteristic Cushitic -n plural suffix invites a more crucial question as to the origin of this element, for, except for this (in place of which proto-Semitic has -$\bar{u}$), a common conjugational system could be postulated for both families. However, with reflexes in the mutually remote Arabic and Northern Gurage, it appears that an -n having the appropriate distribution requires recognition in the proto-Semitic system. Conjugations having an -n suffixed to the characteristic 2/3 (mas.) plural marker -$\bar{u}$, have an -u suffix in the remaining forms. It is argued that these are allomorphs in complementary distribution. Only main verbs are marked with -u/-n, but the modal distinction carried in Arabic and Soddo seems to be relatively weak and this may explain why it has not persisted in Cushitic (see below, however). Consequently the final vocalic (-u) allomorphs eventually disappeared. The consonantal -n persisted, however, acquiring significance as a plural marker. The only post-thematic affixes occurring with subordinate clause verbs were vocalic (Sg.fem. 2 -$\bar{\iota}$, Pl.mas. 2/3 -$\bar{u}$, Pl.fem. 2/3 -$\bar{a}$), and, with an isolated exception, they suffered the fate of modal marker -u. Loss of these elements collapsed the opposition between 2/3 singular and plural forms. Further reductions in the system are explained in terms of levelling.

Whilst reflecting on this attractive hypothesis this reader felt the need of considering certain questions invited by it. The first of these concerns the absence of -n in the Sg.fem. 2 in Beja — the author himself draws attention to this (p. 279). However, it seems very unlikely that -n would be retained with a singular form after it had acquired the specific meaning of a plural marker. A more searching question concerns the disappearance of the archaic plural marker -$\bar{u}$ in Cushitic. The author adduces some evidence for its persistence in the form of the dialectal alternants Pl. 2 -tu/-$t\acute{a}ni$, Pl. 3 -u/-$\acute{a}ni$ in Galla. But this unique preservation of -$\bar{u}$ word-finally is scarcely as remarkable as its wholesale disappearance from forms where it would have been "shielded" from "erosion" by the final -n.

It is suggested, however, that there is further evidence not only for -$\bar{u}$ (plural marker) but also for -u (modal marker) in Cushitic. In the paradigm of verbs of the prefix class in ᶜAfar there is a modal conjugation which exactly resembles that reconstructed for proto-Cushitic.[2]

---

[1] In Galla the syncretism is complete; only one form is found.

[2] Tucker terms this a subjunctive. In ᶜAfar this conjugation has a number of functions, none of which is, in any sense, a subjunctive. Tucker A.N., "Fringe Cushitic, an experiment in typological comparison," *BSOAS*, XXX, 1967, 666.

The modal conjugation of *usūl* 'laugh' appears as: Sg. 1 *asālu*, Sg. 2 *tasālu*, Sg.mas. 3 *yasālu*, Sg.fem. 3 *tasālu*, Pl. 1 *nasālu*, Pl. 2 *tasālōnu*, Pl. 3 *yasālōnu*. It is suggested that the -*ōnu* in Pl. 2/3 reflects earlier -*ūn*. (There are other instances in ᶜAfar where a long *ū* is replaced by *ō*[3]). In ᶜAfar-Saho a non-modal post-thematic suffix -*e* (originally perhaps euphonic) occurs with perfect and non-perfect. Interestingly enough, in the emphatic forms of these conjugations the -*e* in Pl. 2/3 forms is long. E.g. *yusūleh* 'he laughed', *yusūlēnih* 'they laughed'. Thus the disappearance of -*ū* could be accounted for as follows:

1. The modal marker allomorph -*n* became recategorized as a plural marker.

2. This paved the way for an identification of -*ū* (ᶜAfar-Saho -*ō*) as an allomorph of modal -*u* — a very reasonable thing in terms of phonetic similarity.

3. Once -*ū* had acquired this role it was inappropriate for it to appear with non-modal forms. In ᶜAfar-Saho, where non-modal forms other than Pl. 2/3 developed an -*e*, levelling took place, so that -*ūn* ﹥ -*ēn*. In Somali, S. Agaw and Galla it cannot be said that the -*ū* undergoes analogical replacement exactly since the vowel of Pl. 2/3 non-modal conjugations is not identical with that found in the remaining forms. Nevertheless, it is true to say that a redistribution of vowels takes place so that -*ū* never precedes the -*n*.

6.   BERBER

6.1. PENCHOEN, THOMAS G., *Tamazight of the Ayt Ndhir.* (Afroasiatic Dialects, Eds. Wolf Leslau and Thomas G. Penchoen, Volume 1). Los Angeles: Undena Publications, 1973, iii, 124 pp.
    By LIONEL GALAND (École Pratique des Hautes Études, Paris)

La nouvelle collection "Afroasiatic Dialects," publiée sous la direction de MM. W. Leslau et T.G. Penchoen, a pour objet la "description concise" de langues ou de parlers appartenant à la famille "afroasiatique," appellation à laquelle on préfère en France celle de "chamito-sémitique," plus ancienne, plus arbitraire et, par là même, moins exposée à des interprétations erronées. Depuis l'*Essai comparatif* de Marcel Cohen (1947), qui reste un ouvrage classique, la comparaison dans ce domaine a fait des progrès certains, moins peut-être par les travaux qu'elle a suscités que par l'intérêt désormais affirmé qu'elle éveille chez les divers spécialistes: on a pu le vérifier à l'occasion du deuxième congrès international de linguistique chamito-sémitique, tenu à Florence en avril 1974. Bien que le cas des langues tchadiennes reste réservé, on est déjà loin du temps où l'existence même de la famille chamito-sémitique n'était qu'une hypothèse de travail. Mais, pour être fructueuse, la comparaison doit reposer sur une connaissance suffisante de chacune des langues du group. Tous les secteurs n'ont pas été également explorés, tant s'en faut, et l'on éprouve le besoin de faire le point. La série AAD vient donc à son heure.

---

[3]The final -*u* in *tasālōnu* and *yasālōnu* is a phonologically required element and is not original.

C'est le berbère qui a l'honneur d'ouvrir la voie, l'ouvrage de M.P. étant consacré au parler
des Ayt Ndhir du Maroc central. Ce parler constitue avec beaucoup d'autres un important
groupe dialectal auquel les locuteurs, qui se nomment *imaziɣn* "Berbères," donnent le nom de
ṯamaziɣṯ. La variété propre aux Ayt Ndhir avait jadis été étudiée par Abès, *Première année
de langue berbère (dialecte du Maroc central)*, Rabat, 1916, par E. Laoust, *Cours de berbère
marocain: dialectes du Maroc central*, Rabat 1924 (avec rééditions), et, plus systématique-
ment, par P. Bisson, *Leçons de berbère tamazight: dialecte des Aït Ndhir (Aït Naaman)*, Rabat,
1940, mais aucun de ces travaux ne présentait la rigueur souhaitable. La tamazight connaît
encore la faveur des chercheurs, puisque le livre de M.P. a été précédé par ceux de M. E.T.
Abdel-Massih, *Tamazight Verb Structure: a Generative Approach*, Indiana University, 1968,— A
Course in Spoken Tamazight, Ann Arbor, 1971, — A *Reference Grammar of Tamazight*, Ann Arbor,
1971, — et suivi par celue de Mme J. Harries, *Tamazight Basic Course*, Madison, 1974; Mme H.
avait déjà étudié ces parlers dans une thèse restée inédite; in outre, les éléments méridionaux
du groupe ont fait l'objet d'une enquête récente de M. A.Willms, *Grammatik der südlichen Ber-
aberdialekte (Südmarokko)*, Hamburg, 1972.

Le travail de M.P. reste essentiellement descriptif, mais l'auteur a eu la sagesse de ne pas
se priver de l'aide que peut apporter la comparaison interdialectale. On lui saura gré de ne
s'être laissé enfermer dans aucun dogmatisme d'école. Il s'efforce d'analyser les faits et non
de les faire entrer dans des formules toutes prêtes. Élégante et claire, sa description
atteint la précision voulue sans donner dans le jargon à la mode. La discussion de certains
points accessoires ou trop complexes est rejetée dans des notes au bas des pages et le texte
principal y gagne en légèreté. Le désir d'être simple est si manifeste qu'on se demande parfois
si la difficulté a été esquivée pour le confort du lecteur ou si l'auteur l'a réellement oub-
liée. Les matériaux berbères ont été recueillis avec soin et paraissent sûrs.

Après avoir fourni quelques indications générales sur le berbère, M.P. dégage, pour l'essentiel,
le système phonologique du parler des Ayt Ndhir (chap. 2). Sauf cas particulier, toute occlusive
non tendue devient ici spirante. Le phénomène n'a pas la même ampleur dans toute la tamazight,
malgré ce que pourrait laisser croire la rédaction du §2.2.1: chez les Ayt Youssi d'Enjil,
par exemple, les dentales ne sont pas atteintes. M.P. accorde avec raison beaucoup d'importance à l'opposition de tension, mais il se laisse influencer par la morphologie (donc par l'
histoire, dans une certaine mesure) quand il hésite à reconnaître le plein statut de phonèmes
tendus à /ɣɣ/, /ww/, /yy/ (note 2 des pp. 5 et 7): certes les correspondants tendus de /ɣ/,
/w/, /y/, dans la morphologie, sont plus souvent /qq/, /ggʷ/, /gg/, que /ɣɣ/, /ww/, /yy/, mais
cette correspondance n'est que l'héritage d'un système phonologique antérieur. On n'hésitera
pas à écrire *iyya*, *aɣɣu*, si telles sont bien les réalisations. Le parler s'est donné de
nouveaux phonèmes tendus /ɣɣ/, /ww/, /yy/, de même qu'il s'est donné de nouveaux phonèmes non
tendus /ṯ/, /g/ (occlusif), /q/, etc., qui ne sont du reste pas tous dux aux emprunts comme
pourrait le faire croire le §2.2.2: v. *aqmu* 'bouche'. Inversement, peut-être ne faudrait-il
pas négliger l'histoire au point de dire (p. 8, §g) que la séquence /y/ + /wašal/ 'devient'
[ggʷašæl]: [ggʷ] ne s'explique ici que par référence à l'époque où la préposition était encore
/g/; la combinaison /gg/ (< /g/ + /w/) a été conservée alors que /g/, dans d'autres environ-
nements, passait localement à /g̱/, puis à /y/.

M.P. est d'accord avec tous les berbérisants actuels pour dénombrer en tamazight trois phonèmes
vocaliques /a/, /i/, /u/. Il admet sans difficulté (p. 10) le caractère purement phonétique
de la voyelle centrale [ə] et surtout en appendice (pp. 94-95), il fournit un effort original
(déjà tenté par M. Abdel-Massih, mais sur d'autres bases) pour décrire les réalisations de
cette voyelle. Il en indique aussi les pseudo-réalisations: là où l'on croyait entendre [ə],
on n'a souvent, en réalité, que l'explosion d'une occlusive ou l'emploi d'une consonne (/n/,
/r/, etc.) comme centre de syllabe. Je soutiens cette idée depuis trop longtemps pour ne pas
me réjouir de cette vérification, mais il est dommage que M.P. ait continué à employer le
même signe ə pour noter des phénomènes aussi divers, ce qui expose son lecteur (sauf pour quelques pages de l'appendice) aux dangers que présentaient les anciennes graphies.

L'étude morphologique (chapitre 3) porte d'abord sur le nom et présente clairement les oppositions de genre, de nombre et d'état. Malgré le succès du pluriel en -*n*, il n'est peut-être

pas opportun de le désigner comme le type de base ("basic regular pattern," p. 14), non plus
que de proposer une analyse "de surface" *i-maksa-wan* (p. 15) pour la contester ensuite (p.
16 et note 8). — A propos de l'état, l'auteur distingue les noms dont la voyelle initiale
est un préfixe de genre et de nombre et ceux dont la voyelle initiale apartiendrait au radical (p. 13). La réalité est sans doute plus complexe, mais cette distinction allège la description des mécanismes qui précisément l'ont suggérée. Les tableaux dressés par M.P. sont
très parlants (pp. 20-21); toutefois ils ne différencient pas les formes réeles et les formes
reconstituées, comme *wa-ryaz*, *wa-maziɣ*, etc., dont on ne sait se elles ont pour l'auteur
une valeur historique ou simplement didactique. Nulle mention n'est faite—et c'est un peu
injuste—de l'article d'A. Basset, "Sur la voyelle initiale en berbère" (repris dans *Articles
de dialectologie berbère*, 1959), qui fut le premier à démonter, en 1945, les rouages de
l'opposition d'état.

Viennent ensuite les sections consacrées aux éléments démonstratifs, aux noms de nombres, aux
pronoms personnels, aux prépositions et au verbe. Ce dernier constitue toujours un chapitre
difficile de la morphologie berbère. M.P. se tire de l'épreuve avec honneur. A l'aide de
tableaux bien composés et commentés avec précision, il sait conduire le lecteur dans le dédale
des diverses formations, après avoir présenté les grandes lignes du système verbal. Il propose
de reconnaître deux grands "axes de contraste," imparfait—parfait et événement ("event")—
extension, qui permettent les oppositions aspectuelles (p. 29). L'expression de l'imparfait est
confiée, pour noter l'événement, au thème "non marqué" (l'aoriste d'A. Basset, qui parlait
déjà de "terme non marqué": LB, p. 14) précédé de la particule "projective" *ad*, et, pour
noter l'extension, au thème "intensif" (l'aoriste intensif d'A. Basset) précédé de *ad*. Le
domaine du parfait appartient, pour l'événement, au thème du "parfait" (le prétérit d'A. Basset)
et, pour l'extension, au thème "intensif" précédé d'une particule *la*, *da* ou *ar*. On voit que
la description opère sur des syntagmes plutôt que sur les formes verbales proprement dites,
puisque les particules y jouent un rôle décisif. D'autre part l'opposition entre événement
et extension n'est pas très clair: un événement répété, par exemple, entre dans le domaine de
l'extension. Mais ce qui paraît franchement contestable, c'est le rôle attribué à l'intensif
dans l'expression du parfait, à moins qu'il ne faille donner à ce nom de "parfait" un sens qui
m'échappe (l'auteur étant trop averti, par ailleurs, pour avoir commis une confusion avec le
"passé"). J'ai tenté de montrer (en premier lieu dans l'*Annuaire 1972/1973 de l'École pratique
des hautes études*, Paris, 1973, pp. 175-176) que l'aoriste intensif est aujourd'hui la seule
forme verbale à posséder en propre la valeur d'un "inaccompli," nom que je préfère lui donner
désormais; c'est donc lui qui s'oppose directement au prétérit ou "accompli." Il est vrai que
l'aoriste simple, aujourd'hui "non marqué," représente sans doute un ancien inaccompli, mais
par lui-même il n'a plus cette valeur et il ne peut l'assumer qu'à la faveur de certaines
combinaisons syntaxiques. Dans le rôle de l'inaccompli, il a cédé la place à l'"intensif,"
ancienne forme dérivée qui a cessé d'être traitée comme telle. La morphologie conserve le
souvenir d'un système verbal aujourd'hui dépassé.

Le chapitre 4 est consacré à la syntaxe et d'abord à la phrase verbale. La description part,
très judicieusement, du type fondamental illustré par *idda uryaz* 'il-est-parti homme' =
'l'homme est parti'. Comme *idda* 'il est parti' peut constituer à lui seul un énoncé gram-
maticalement complet, j'ai proposé de voir dans *uryaz* un "complément explicatif" développant
l'indice de personne *i-*; cette analyse, corroborée par certains emplois de l'état d'annexion
en kabyle, permet un usage cohérent du terme "sujet," que l'on peut alors réserver à l'indice
(ici *i*) obligatoirement présent dans l'énoncé verbal. M.P. ne pose pas le problème et il
conserve pour *uryaz* l'appellation traditionnelle de "sujet." Du moins renonce-t-il avec raison
à étendre cette appellation au cas où le nom passe avant le verbe: *aryaz idda* 'homme il-
est-parti' = 'l'homme, il est parti' et je ne peux que souscrire à ce qu'il dit (p. 76 et
suiv.) de l'indicateur de thème ("topicalized noun") et de la mise en relief ("clefting").

La description de la phrase nominale (p. 61 et suiv.) ne fait aucune mention de la particule
prédicative *d* "c'est", que les parlers voisins emploient beaucoup dans des énoncés du type
X *d* Y "X est Y" et que P. Bisson signale précisément chez les Ayt Ndhir. Serait-on en
présence d'un phénomène propre au parler local décrit par M.P.? Il est dommage que ce dernier

ne se soit pas expliqué là-dessus par référence à Bisson. Par ailleurs je ne suis toujours pas
convaincu de l'intérêt que présente pour le linguiste soucieux d'observer les faits la ré-
duction des phrases nominales à des phrases à verbe "être," fût-ce au nom d'une structure
profonde (p. 62).

A propos du syntagme nominal (p. 63 et suiv.), on notera qu'aucune trace de la préposition *n*
"de" n'apparaît, non seulement dans *axam uryaz* 'la tente de l'homme', ce qui est courant, mais
dans *taduṭṭ wulli* 'la laine des moutons', où l'on pourrait attendre *uwulli* < *n* + *wulli*. Si
les notations de M.P. sont correctes (et c'est un auteur qui note bien), il y aurait là un
argument en faveur de la thèse, soutenue par A. Basset, selon laquelle le berbère conserve
avec certains noms une construction non prépositionnelle du complément déterminatif; le fait
que la présence ou l'absence de n soit conditionnée par l'environnement phonique me laisse
croire, cependant, que de tels exemples résultent plutôt d'evolutions relativement récentes.

L'étude du syntagme nominal appelait celle de la proposition relative. M.P. la décrit très
nettement (p. 67 et suiv.). Le berbère n'ayant pas de pronoms relatifs, il est malaisé de
trouver une terminologie adéquate pour distinguer les relatives du type "qui," du type "que,"
etc. L'auteur recourt aux expressions "subject relative clause," "direct object relative
clause," etc., qui, prises à la lettre, sont impropres, mais que le lecteur comprendra sans
peine.

Une attention particulière est accordée aux cas où une proposition peut commuter avec un groupe
nominal (p. 71 et suiv.), ce qui donne lieu à une série d'observations intéressantes. Il me
semble toutefois que la tournure *ibda ar issawal* 'il commença il parlait' = 'il se mit à
parler' (p. 73) s'explique plutôt par une parataxe que par l'emploi de *ar issawal* comme complément d'object direct de *ibda*.

La description est illustrée par un conte (chapitre 5), publié avec une traduction littérale
et une traduction courante. Des appendices (chapitre 6) complètent les données sur la morpho-
ogie du verbe. Le chapitre 7 réunit le vocabulaire correspondant aux listes établies par M.
Swadesh pour la glottochronologie (sur laquelle M.P. formule néanmoins des réserves), ce qui
facilitera certaines comparaisons. Le tableau de l'alphabet touareg (chapitre 8) satisfera
la curiosité des lecteurs, mais, en fait, il ne concerne pas la tamazight. Conformément au
plan proposé par les responsables de la collection (v. page 4 de la couverture), le chapitre 9
rappelle et définit la terminologie employée dans le cours de l'ouvrage. Enfin le chapitre 10
est une bibliographie. L'auteur la destine surtout aux étudiants (p. 117) et, renvoyant à des
travaux plus détaillés, il l'a volontairement réduite. Mais les principes qui ont guidé son
choix n'apparaissent pas toujours clairement: il mentionne l'étude de M. Abdel-Massih sur
le verbe, mais ne cite ni la grammaire, ni le cours de tamazight (v. ci-dessus); il nomme un
seul des deux "Cours" de Laoust, et c'est, curieusement,) celui de chleuh (v. ci-dessus); il
renvoie à divers articles d'E. Destaing, mais passe sous silence le travail d'A. Basset sur
la voyelle initiale du nom (v. ci-dessus), ainsi que mon analyse de la mise en relief (*Mémor-
ial André Basset,* 1957), dont il accepte pourtant les conclusions, etc. On ne peut sans
quelque gêne simplifier ce qui est complexe. Mais en fin de compte M.P. a réussi: son livre
guidera l'étudiant, renseignera le comparatiste et fera réfléchir le berbérisant. C'est un
heureux début pour Afroasiatic Dialects.

La présentation matérielle est dépourvue de luxe, mais concourt à la clarté de l'ouvrage:
format agréable et favorable aux tableaux (21,5 x 28 cm), caractères un peu petits, mais très
lisibles, à espacement plus grand dans les mots berbères, ce qui a permis de renoncer aux
italiques. A la liste des corrections proposées aux pp. 123-124, on pourra ajouter: p. 86, 1.
2, *yiwəṭ-ṭ*, et non γ-; p. 87, 1. 38, 'they exit', et non 'exist'; p. 107, n° 80, *asəy*, et non
asi (cf. p. 31, §a, 1. 5); p. 108, 1. 3, *tifinaγ*, et non *tifanaγ*.

7. APPENDIX

**7.1. Proposed Constitution for the North-American Conference on Afroasiatic Linguistics.
By Giorgio Buccellati.**

(As indicated in the Preamble, the author was charged at the last meeting of NACAL in Columbus, Ohio, to prepare the draft of a constitution for the future activities of the Conference. Such proposed text is appended below, and will serve as a basis for discussion at the next meeting which will be held in Philadelphia, Pennsylvania.)

7.1.1. PREAMBLE

The conference was started in 1973, when the first meeting was held at Santa Barbara, California, on March 24-25; it was organized by Robert Hetzron of the University of California, Santa Barbara, in cooperation with Giorgio Buccellati of the University of California, Los Angeles, and Joseph L. Malone of Barnard College-Columbia University. The second meeting was also held in Santa Barbara, on March 25-26 1974; it was organized by Gene Gragg of the University of Chicago in cooperation with Robert Hetzron. The third meeting was held in Columbus, Ohio, on April 22-23, 1975; it was organized by Frederic J. Cadora of Ohio State University.

The name of the Conference has been, during the first three meetings, North American Conference on Semitic Linguistics. Already during the second meeting, however, the participants agreed that it was preferable to opt for a broader scope as reflected in the name North American Conference on Afroasiatic Linguistics. This is now adopted as the regular name of the Conference. The numbering of the meetings will however continue in sequence, so that the next meeting will be known as the fourth meeting of the North American Conference of Afroasiatic Linguistics.

At the Columbus Conference an organizational meeting of the participants resulted in a few informal resolutions listed below.

(1) The Conference should continue on a regular basis. There should be enough structure to ensure its survival, yet it should not become overbureaucratized (to avoid, for instance, having to impose dues on members).

(2) There should be a representative body of scholars to give it a sense of direction and continuity. At the same time, there should be as much room as possible for individual initiative and leadership.

(3) The five individuals who have been responsible for the organization of the first three Conferences should draw up a document defining the nature and procedures of the Conference. Giorgio Buccellati was asked to serve as coordinator.

(4) Various suggestions were advanced with regard to procedures, e.g. the use of prepring papers was encouraged, and so was the scheduling of the Conference at the same general time as the AOS meeting, although it was strongly felt that there should be no overlap in the presentation of papers.

7.1.2. GOALS

The aim of the Conference is to promote the interest of Semitist and other Afroasiatic area specialists in the various modern currents of linguistics. Conversely, the Conference will also draw the attention of general linguists to Afroasiatic data. Specific fields of interest may be classified under the headings of synchronic description, historical reconstruction, comparatism and contributions of general linguistics to Afroasiatic and vice versa.

7.1.3. MEMBERSHIP

Any interested individual or institution may become a member of the Conference by submitting name and address to the Executive Secretary.

Privileges of membership entail simply being placed on the Conference mailing list, as a result of which a member will receive notices of meetings and other pertinent communications.

While the Conference is meant to serve especially the needs of North American scholars, membership of other foreign individuals and institutions is welcomed.

7.1.4. POLICY COMMITTEE

Scholarly responsibility for the Conference rests with the Policy Committee. Its functions are to define the role of the Conference, its scholarly orientation, its organizational structure, and the like. It also appoints from year to year the Executive Secretary of the Conference.

The Committee consists of an open number of scholars, who will reflect a general balance in terms of area specialization within Afroasiatic and geographical distribution within North America.

The first Policy Committee consists of the five individuals who organized the first three meetings of the Conference. Rejuvenation is in the hands of the Committee itself: new members will be coopted upon a simple majority vote; existing members will terminate their tenure upon resignation or simple majority vote.

Contacts among members of the Policy Committee will normally be initiated by the Executive Secretary. It is expected that decisions may normally be reached by mail, without the need of actual meetings.

7.1.5. EXECUTIVE SECRETARY

Organizational responsibility for the Conference rests with the Executive Secretary. Besides initiating contacts among the members of the Policy Committee, the Secretary's main function is to plan and coordinate the annual meeting of the Conference.

The executive Secretary is appointed yearly by the Policy Committee, of which he is an ex officio member.

7.1.6. BUDGET

Funds for the printing and mailing of notices, as well as for general correspondence, are to be found on ad hoc basis. It is expected that normal costs may be absorbed through existing channels, such as the academic institutions of the Executive Secretary and other members of the Policy Committee, or the administrative office of the journal *Afroasiatic Linguistics*.

SOURCES AND MONOGRAPHS ON THE ANCIENT NEAR EAST

Editors: Giorgio Buccellati, Marilyn Kelly Buccellati, Piotr Michalowski

These two series make available original documents in English translation (*Sources*) and important studies by modern scholars (*Monographs*) as a contribution to the study of history, religion, literature, art and archaeology of the Ancient Near East. Inexpensive and flexible in format, they are meant to serve the specialist by bringing within easy reach basic publications often in updated versions, to provide imaginative educational outlets for undergraduate and graduate courses, and to reach the interested segments of the educated lay audience.

General Subscription — For a prepayment of $10 the subscriber selects random issues from within the entire system as desired, up to a total of 200 pages. The subscriber is also entitled to (1) periodical lists of abstracts from both series, and (2) reservation to given categories to be specified by the subscriber (e.g. Assyriology or Egyptology).

Library Subscription — the subscription price is $8 for Volume 1 of either the *Sources* or the *Monographs*. A volume will average 200 pages. Periodicity in the order of appearance of fascicles is not predetermined, but a volume will normally be completed within one year.

Sources from the Ancient Near East

Volume 1

- 1. *The Akkadian Namburbi Texts: an Introduction.* By R. I. Caplice. 24 pp., $1.00

- 2. *Balag-Compositions: Sumerian Lamentation Liturgies of the Second and First Millennium B.C.* By M. E. Cohen. 32 pp., $2.40

Monographs on the Ancient Near East

Volume 1

- 1. *The Sumerian Temple City.* By A. Falkenstein. Introduction and translation by M. Dej. Ellis. 21 pp., 95¢

- 2. *Three Essays on the Sumerians.* By B. Landsberger. Introduction and translation by M. Dej. Ellis. 18 pp., 90¢

- 3. *Structure of Society and State in Early Dynastic Sumer.* By I. B. Diakonoff. Introduction by M. Desrochers 16 pp., 65¢

- 4. *The Conceptual Autonomy of the Babylonian World.* By B. Landsberger. Translation by Th. Jacobsen, B. Foster and H. von Siebenthal. Introduction by Th. Jacobsen. 16 pp., $1.10

All prices are postpaid. Payment must accompany orders from individuals. A handling fee of 80¢ will be charged to libraries if order is not prepaid. Discount of 20 % on all orders received within one year of publication date. Order from: UNDENA PUBLICATIONS, P. O. B. 97, Malibu, California 90265, U.S.A.

AFROASIATIC DIALECTS

A series of grammars providing concise descriptions of individual languages within the Afroasiatic family, and directed to scholars and students in the given language areas as well as in linguistics.

Editors: Wolf Leslau and Thomas G. Penchoen

- Volume 1 (Berber). *Tamazight of the Ayt Ndhir.* By Thomas G. Penchoen. 124 pp. $8.50.

- Volume 2 (Ancient Egyptian). *Middle Egyptian.* By John B. Callender. 150 pp. $10.00.

○ Volume 3 (Semitic). *Damascus Arabic.* By Arne Ambros. In preparation.

BIBLIOTHECA MESOPOTAMICA

Primary sources and interpretive analyses for the study of Mesopotamian civilization and its influences from late prehistory to the end of the cuneiform tradition.

- Volume 1. *Old Sumerian and Old Akkadian Texts in Philadelphia Chiefly from Nippur.*
  Part 1. Literary and Lexical Texts and the Earliest Administrative Documents from Nippur.
  By Aage Westenholz. xii-210 pp., 3 plates. $18.50 (hardbound), $12 (softbound).

- Volume 2. *Babylonian Planetary Omens. Part 1. The Venus Tablet of Ammisaduqa.*
  By Erica Reiner in collaboration with David Pingree. Approx. 60 pp. $6.75.

In preparation:

○ *Texts from al-Hiba-Lagash.* By Robert D. Biggs.

○ *Soil and Salinity in Ancient Mesopotamia.* By Thorkild Jacobsen.

Old Sumerian and Old Akkadian Texts in Philadelphia. By Aage Westenholz.
○ *Part 2. Late Sargonic Administrative Texts from Nippur: 'Akkadian' Texts, Legal Documents and the Onion Archive.*
○ *Part 3. Late Sargonic Administrative Texts from Nippur: Ration Lists and Miscellaneous Accounts.*
○ *Part 4. Presargonic and Sargonic Administrative Texts from Fara and Ur.*

○ *The Economic Role of the Crown in the Old Babylonian Period.* By Norman Yoffee.